Lost in Translation

D1610571

American Indies

Series Editors: Gary Needham and Yannis Tzioumakis

Titles in the series include:

Lost in Translation
Geoff King
978 0 7486 3745 4 (hbk)
978 0 7486 3746 1 (pbk)

The Spanish Prisoner
Yannis Tzioumakis
978 0 7486 3368 5 (hbk)
978 0 7486 3369 2 (pbk)

Brokeback Mountain
Gary Needham
978 0 7486 3382 1 (hbk)
978 0 7486 3383 8 (pbk)

Forthcoming titles include:

Far From Heaven
Glyn Davis
978 0 7486 3778 2 (hbk)
978 0 7486 3779 9 (pbk)

Memento
Claire Molloy
978 0 7486 3771 3 (hbk)
978 0 7486 3772 0 (pbk)

Lost in Translation

Geoff King

Edinburgh University Press

Edinburgh University Press Ltd
22 George Square, Edinburgh

www.euppublishing.com

Typeset in 11/13pt Monotype Baskerville by
Servis Filmsetting Ltd, Stockport, Cheshire, and
printed and bound in Great Britain by
CPI Antony Rowe, Chippenham and Eastbourne

A CIP record for this book is available from the British Library

ISBN 978 0 7486 3745 4 (hardback)
ISBN 978 0 7486 3746 1 (paperback)

Contents

Series Preface

In recent years American independent cinema has not only become the focus of significant scholarly attention but as a category of film it has shifted from a marginal to a central position within American cinema – a shift that can be also detected in the emergence of the label 'indie' cinema as opposed to independent cinema. The popularisation of this 'indie' brand of filmmaking began in the 1990s with the commercial success of the Sundance Film Festival and of specialty distributor Miramax Films, as well as the introduction of DVD, which made independent films more readily available as well as profitable for the first time. At the same time, film studies started developing courses that distinguished American independent cinema from mainstream Hollywood, treating it as a separate object of study and a distinct discursive category.

Despite the surge in interest in independent cinema, a surge that involved the publication of at least twenty books and edited collections alongside a much larger number of articles on various aspects of independent cinema, especially about the post-1980 era, the field – as it has developed – still remains greatly under-researched in relation to the changes of the past twenty years that define the shift from independent to 'indie' cinema. This is partly because a multifaceted phenomenon such as American independent cinema, the history of which is as long and complex as the history of mainstream Hollywood, has yet to be adequately and satisfactorily documented. In this respect, academic film criticism is still in great need to account for the plethora of shapes, forms and guises that American independent cinema has manifested itself in. This is certainly not an easy task given that independent film has, indeed, taken a wide variety of forms at different historical trajectories and has been influenced by a hugely diverse range of factors.

It is with this problem in mind that 'American Indies' was conceived by its editors. While the history of American independent cinema is still being written with more studies already set to be published in the forth-coming years, and while journal articles are enhancing our understand-ing of more focused aspects of independent filmmaking, the 'American Indies' series has been created to provide the necessary space to explore and engage with specific examples of American 'indie' films in a great depth. Through this format, 'American Indies' aims to encourage an examination of both the 'indie' text and its contexts, of understanding how 'indie' films operate within a particular filmmaking practice but also how 'indies' have been shaping a new formation of American cinema. In this respect, 'American Indies' provides the space for a detailed examina-tion of industrial, economic and institutional concerns alongside the more usual formal and aesthetic considerations that have historically charac-terised critical approaches of independent films. 'American Indies' is a series of comprehensive studies of carefully selected examples of recent films that reveal in great detail the many sides of the phenomenon of the recently emerged American 'indie' cinema.

As the first book series to explore and define this aspect of American cinema, 'American Indies' has had the extremely difficult task of pro-ducing a comprehensive set of criteria that informs its selection of titles. Given the vastness of the field, we have made several editorial decisions in order to produce a coherent definition of this new phase of American independent cinema. The first such choice was to concentrate on recent examples of independent cinema. Although the word 'recent' has often been used to include films made in the post-1980 period, as editors we decided that the cut off point for films to be included in this series would be the year 1996. This was an extremely significant year in the inde-pendent film sector, 'the year of the independents' as was triumphantly proclaimed by the *Los Angeles Business Journal* in February 1997, for a number of reasons. Arguably, the most significant of these reasons was the dynamic entrance in the film market of Fox Searchlight, a new type of a specialty film division created by 20th Century Fox in 1995 with the explicit intention of claiming a piece of the increasingly large inde-pendent film market pie. Fox Searchlight would achieve this objective through the production and distribution of films that followed many of the conventions of independent film as those were established after the success of *sex, lies and videotape* in 1989. These conventions had since then started being popularised by a number of films produced and distributed by Miramax Films, an independent company that was taken over by Disney after the phenomenal box-office success of several of its films at approximately the same time as 20th Century Fox was establishing its specialty division.

The now direct involvement of entertainment conglomerates like Disney and Fox in the independent film sector had far-reaching effects. Arguably, the most important of these was that the label 'independent', which for critics and the cinema going public (wrongly) signified economic independence from major film companies like Disney, Fox, Paramount, Universal, etc., obviously ceased to convey this meaning. Instead, critics and public alike started using increasingly the label 'indie' which suggested a particular type of film that adhered to a set of conventions as well as a transformed independent cinema sector that was now driven by specialty companies, most of which subsidiaries of major entertainment conglomerates. It is this form of 'independent' cinema that has produced some of the most interesting films to come out from American cinema in recent years that 'American Indies' has set out to explore in great depth and which explains our selection of the label 'indies' instead of 'independents'.

We hope readers will enjoy the series

Gary Needham and Yannis Tzioumakis
American Indies Series Editors

Introduction

Lost in Translation opens with a fade-up from black to a medium close-up shot of Scarlet Johansson's rear, clad in transparent pastel pink underwear, as her character lies down on her side. The image, framing her figure from lower back to just below the knee, is held for a lengthy thirty-four seconds and largely abstracted from the narrative at the time; still at first, then moving slightly as the legs adjust position. Company credits fade in and out above the upper edge of the figure, followed by music and the appearance of the main title across the lower half of her body, before the image fades again to black and the film proper seems to begin. The opening sets the tone of the piece, particularly in its languorous and softly glowing qualities, but also grated for some viewers, the overt nature of its display of the female body seeming out of keeping with the more general tenor of the film, even if the character does remain scantily clad in a number of scenes that follow. The location of the image, detached and at the privileged opening moment, gives it what appears to be an emblematic quality; but emblematic of what, exactly?

The impression is marked as one that seems designed to be 'seductive', in a manner that mixes more and less subtle qualities (more so in the image texture and the leisurely way in which it is presented; less in the close-to-nude status of the lower regions of a body that seems all the more objectified in being removed from its head or its location at this stage in relation to an identifiable character). If the opening is emblematic of anything, it might be of the status of *Lost in Translation* more generally, in its particular location in the wider cinematic spectrum. It offers, on the one hand, an 'obvious' point of appeal, in its potentially erotic dimension and the proximity of the bodily spectacle to the camera, although this is combined with what might be considered to be more 'subtle' aesthetic qualities and an 'artistic' point of reference (I am putting such terms within quotation marks to suggest that these are marked positionings or

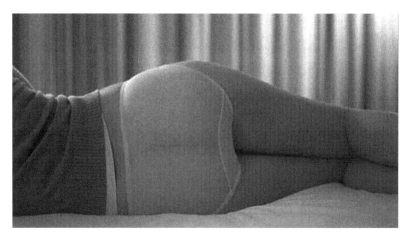

Figure 1 'Seductive' qualities: the opening image of *Lost in Translation*. © 2003 Universal Studios

accents rather than inherent or self-evident qualities). For those in the know, the image is based on the paintings of the American photorealist John Kacere, a source acknowledged by the filmmaker, which include numerous similarly framed pictures of scantily clad female mid-sections, although Kacere's work seems more blatantly sexist in orientation (garish in quality and often combining such underwear with other flimsy garments, while Johansson's character, Charlotte, mixes hers with a more 'sensible' jumper). This combination of qualities is in some respects typical of the film as a whole, and the manner in which it can be understood to be positioned as an example of American independent or indie cinema.

Lost in Translation is marked as clearly distinctive from the commercial mainstream in a number of dimensions, while also offering some more familiar or conventional points of orientation. The principal aim of this book is to analyse this particular balance of qualities in detail, to pin down what exactly might be the basis of the film's appeal – and its considerable commercial success – and how exactly this locates it in a part of the contemporary indie sector that combines features that might in some cases be associated with 'art' cinema with others closer to what is usually expected of the Hollywood mainstream. I am using expressions such as what might be 'associated with' or 'expected of' the mainstream to underline the extent to which 'the mainstream' itself can be a problematic category, often used in an unexamined manner as a negative reference point for various degrees of alternative production. The Hollywood mainstream is, certainly, a globally dominant industrial phenomenon that represents an inescapable point of departure for many other kinds of cinema, but the degree to which it offers an entirely homogenous point of comparison is easily overstated. The perspective adopted in this book seeks to chart a dynamic series of relationships between elements drawn from different kinds of cinema, including those generally recognised as mainstream and others, institutionalised in their own ways, such as 'art' or 'indie' cinema. The position occupied by an individual example such as *Lost in Translation* can be understood as the outcome of a series of forces within what Pierre Bourdieu terms the 'field of cultural production', the wider network of objective relationships that creates the context within which any cultural product is likely to become funded, produced, distributed and consumed.[1]

Lost in Translation was generally acknowledged to have been one of the indie hits of 2003–04, earning widespread critical praise and awards, the latter including an Oscar for best original screenplay. I am taking 'indie' here to signify a particular variety of American independent feature production and distribution that became institutionalised and came to prominence during the 1980s and especially from the early 1990s, as opposed to a broader or more literal definition of 'independence' that might include all non-Hollywood output in the history of film in the US, ranging from the avant-garde to various forms of exploitation cinema and also, in some accounts, including certain features that otherwise appear to be solidly in the commercial mainstream.[2] While some have argued that independent status can only be measured at the industrial level, in terms of economic freedom from the Hollywood studio system or any of its offshoots, I suggest that it can also be understood at the level of the substantive material of the films themselves – their form and content – even if this remains an inexact science. Indie or independent are best used as relative terms rather than absolutes, signifying a range of degrees of departure at each level from what might conventionally be expected of work situated in the Hollywood mainstream. This approach is vindicated, I would suggest, by a close study of *Lost in Translation*, a film the status of which might be considered to vary, if a monolithic approach were sought, depending on exactly which of its facets were under examination at any particular moment.

Precisely how *Lost in Translation* is situated at the industrial level is the subject of the first chapter of this book, which traces a movement from more distinctly indie dimensions to others in which the film can also be located in the region known as Indiewood, in which the lines between Hollywood and the independent sector are considerably less clear-cut. The distinction between indie and Indiewood can itself be a blurry one, as evidenced by an analysis of the various dimensions of Coppola's film, hence the use on some occasions in this book of formulations such as 'indie or Indiewood' or 'indie/Indiewood'. This chapter examines the manner in which the film was conceived and financed and strategies employed in distribution and marketing, along with some considera- tion of the initial critical reception. The marketing of the film revolved to a large extent around the presence of Bill Murray in one of the two leading roles, a dimension considered in greater detail in Chapter 2, which examines some of the key frameworks within which the film might be situated for viewers: stardom, the presence of the filmmaker Sofia Coppola as a distinctive 'auteur', and the role of genre, particularly romantic comedy, as a category in relation to which *Lost in Translation* might more ambiguously be located. The formal texture of the film, analysed in Chapter 3, is another key aspect of its positioning, one of the dimensions in which it most clearly makes its claim to a distinctively indie/alternative status, with its low-key approach to narrative and a number of audio-visual strategies that combine to create a particular range of 'atmospheric' impressions. The final chapter more briefly examines some of the thematic issues raised by the film, including its portrait of experiences of alienation and disconnection, aspects of *Lost in Translation* that are linked to a number of questions related to the politics of its representations in the realms of race, gender and class formations.

In all of these dimensions, *Lost in Translation* can be understood to be a film aimed, if only implicitly, at a particular range of audience segments, even if this was something its distributors also sought to transcend, in what proved generally to be a successful bid for cross-over success into a wider market. It positions itself as a work designed for an 'implied audi- ence' equipped with the taste preferences and cultural capital requisite to particular realms of the social spectrum, chiefly those conventionally associated with certain portions of the middle or upper-middle classes, issues I have addressed at greater length elsewhere in relation to these regions of the cinematic landscape.[3] That is to say, qualities such as the film's slow pace and relatively uneventful narrative, and its sometimes expressive use of sound and image, are likely to appeal to some viewers and not to others. Just how far that is the case is demonstrated by viewer responses examined in this book via a sample of 1,900 'customer reviews' posted on the website of the online retailer Amazon.com. It is clear from this sample that many viewers appreciated the particular qualities offered by the film, whether this is expressed briefly or in more considered and/or lengthy comments. Many Amazon reviewers respond negatively, however, sometimes strongly and vociferously so. A similar division is found among another 1,694 'user comments' posted on the Internet Movie Database (IMDb). One of the benefits of these sources of feedback is the apparently wide range of viewers they encompasses, especially Amazon, rather than favouring fans or enthusiasts, as is the case with some other web fora.[4] The negative responses are, in their own way, as informative about the particular qualities offered by the film as those which are more positive, throwing into sharp relief the particular terms of engagement requisite to a pleasureable experience. A brief summary of the overall breakdown of the Amazon and IMDb samples is provided near the end of Chapter 1, while more detailed consideration of the Amazon responses is given throughout the book in relation to the various dimensions of the film outlined above.

1. Industrial Contexts: From Indie to Indiewood

Conception, finance, production: A distinctly indie approach

Lost in Translation is rooted, in several respects, in Coppola's own background, a fact that was emphasised in much of the media coverage of the film's release and is a significant dimension of the manner in which it might be positioned in the wider cinematic spectrum. The jet-lagged setting in Tokyo was inspired by her experiences during several years of travel to the city and elsewhere in connection with various aspects of her earlier career (including photography, work in music video, the development of a line of clothing and the promotion of *The Virgin Suicides* [1999]). From this, apparently, came the starting point, a romance of some kind involving two Americans, temporarily detached from routine and beginning to question the directions of their lives during periods of enforced exile and cultural alienation in a luxury Tokyo hotel.[1] The script was written from the start with Murray in mind, as a character (Bob Harris) caught in the uncertainties of a mid-life crisis. This was played in conjunction with aspects of the filmmaker's personal equivalent: an 'early-twenties crisis' undergone by Coppola, a period that included time spent in Tokyo wondering what to do with her future.

The film was clearly marked as a 'personal' project from the beginning, in other words, one aspect of its position towards the indie end of the film spectrum: personal in the sense of its immediate inspiration (travel/jetlag/Tokyo) and the more substantial resonances drawn from a past period of difficulty undergone by the writer-director. The latter, especially, can be understood as a key credential for the ascription of an 'auteur' label to the filmmaker, further supported by certain formal qualities of the text considered in subsequent chapters. Much was made of the connection between Coppola and Charlotte during interviews published during the release of the film, including a degree of physical resemblance between the two, along with the semi-autobiographical nature of aspects of the script. In one heart-to-heart discussion with Bob, for example, Charlotte talks about her uncertainty about the direction of her life, her past having included attempts at writing and photography, the latter being one of the several avenues explored by Coppola before her settled establishment as a filmmaker. 'Everything about it was very personal to me', as Coppola was quoted saying in one generally representative interview.[2] Exactly how far that stretched, in certain aspects of characterisation in particular, became a subject of gossipy debate in some media circles. A number of commentators pointed out that the mannerisms and tone of voice employed by Giovanni Ribisi, in his performance as Charlotte's self-involved photographer husband, John, resembled those of Coppola's then husband, the film and music-video director Spike Jonze (*Being John Malkovich* [1999], *Adaptation* [2002]); the connection was denied by Coppola in interviews although appeared to be confirmed by Ribisi himself (Coppola and Jonze filed for divorce two months after the release of the film).[3]

The first phase of writing, some twenty pages, began after Coppola's return home from the promotion of *The Virgin Suicides* and was followed by a visit to Tokyo in search of further inspiration.[4] An important part in setting the tone of the piece from an early stage was played by a number of ambient mixes put together for Coppola by Brian Reitzell, who worked with the filmmaker on her first feature and became music producer for *Lost in Translation*, to which she listened while writing (for more on the music and its role in the overall impression created by the film, see Chapter 3).[5] The product of the writing phase was an unusually short screenplay, some seventy pages in length, awkwardly less than usual for a feature, and a project that appeared for this and a number of other reasons to be a difficult sell to a financier or distributor. In interviews, Coppola insists that her intention throughout was that the film would only be made if Murray agreed to star. A lengthy period of wooing followed, some five months, Murray being notoriously difficult to contact. The pair eventually met and Murray agreed to play the lead, although Coppola received no more than a verbal commitment from the star.[6] This was, potentially, a major difficulty for the production. The presence of a star of Murray's order (at what can be assumed to have been agreed to be less than his usual fee, for what was envisaged to be a modestly budgeted work) was a key component of the film, from a commercial perspective, highly likely to sell the project to financiers and/or one of the more substantial independent or studio-affiliated 'speciality' distributors (for more on the specific currency of Murray in this arena, see Chapter 2). The absence of a signed contract would be a significant stumbling block, however, in an industry characterised by perceptions of insecurity and demands for the guaranteed presence of confidence-giving 'bankable' elements, even (sometimes especially) at the speciality end of the market. Coppola was encouraged to take the star at his word by fellow director Wes Anderson, in whose *Rushmore* (1998) Murray made a notable indie-oriented appearance, but such reassurances would be unlikely to count for much among the keepers of movie industry purse-strings.[7]

More generally, Coppola envisaged *Lost in Translation* as less than conventional in a number of respects and was keen to maintain control and independence at the level of textual detail. *The Virgin Suicides* had been well received by most critics but performed only modestly, taking less than $5 million at the domestic box office on a budget estimated at $6 million. Despite her 'Hollywood royalty' connections (father Francis Ford Coppola), this was unlikely to translate into much clout with financiers or distributors, particularly in the case of a project that appeared less than feature length and for which no commitment existed on paper from the major star presence. Instead of seeking up-front support from a US distributor, which would be likely to come with many strings attached, Coppola and her agent, Bart Walker from ICM, opted for a traditional route associated with many of the indie 'classics' of the 1980s and early 1990s.[8] Initial funding for production was raised by selling distribution rights separately for a number of overseas territories. The first port of call was Japan itself, where *The Virgin Suicides* had done well and domestic rights to *Lost in Translation* were bought by Tohokushinsha Film Corporation. Pathé followed, with the rights to France. At this point, as Anne Thompson reports in *Filmmaker* magazine, discussions were begun with Focus International, the foreign sales arm of the eventual US distributor, Focus Features. One further deal was apparently required before Focus International agreed to come on board, the sale of Italian rights to Mikado, at which point Focus committed to its share of the $4 million budget.[9] Exactly how much was contributed by each party is unclear, but the advantage of this method was that no single entity was given a controlling influence. This is an important dimension of any claim the film has to independent status at the industrial/economic level, a subject heavily debated in the specialist trade press and in the indie world more generally, even if the film was to be distributed domestically and in much of the world by subsidiaries of a Hollywood studio.

A key question in debates about indie status that focus on the industrial dimension is the point at which a project might gain support (finance or a promise of distribution, or a combination of the two) from any entity with connections to the Hollywood studios. According to one definition, independent status at this level requires no such involvement before the completion of production (and key aspects of post-production such as editing), the film itself thus being created in total separation from studio resources. Any studio-related funding or production, or any up-front guarantee of distribution, is deemed to contravene such a requirement. A fully independent feature, in these terms, might eventually be sold to a Hollywood studio, or a semi-autonomous studio division, but this has to come after the fact, once it is a finished article, in order for there to be no suggestion that studio funds or distribution guarantees might have played a part in shaping (or, more precisely, for many of those engaged in such debates in the indie community, *tainting*) the nature of the product itself. This is a rather restrictive view and somewhat out of touch with significant developments that occurred in the independent landscape after the rapid growth undergone by the sector during the 1990s. At an earlier stage – say, from the mid-1980s – it may have been the case that many or most films celebrated as 'indie' or independent were what are known as 'negative pick-ups', titles bought by distributors after completion. Subsequent competition for product during the 1990s and after created a more complex situation, however, in which distributors, particularly the studio subsidiaries, were increasingly likely to invest to varying degrees in production, as a way to gain an early stake and increased rights of access to the most attractive material.

Lost in Translation clearly does not qualify for the label 'independent' in the purist industrial sense. Focus International, an important part of the initial package of investors in rights to the film, is precisely the kind of company that might be expected to be viewed with suspicion by those who position themselves as defenders of the indie faith: a division of NBC Universal, one of the major Hollywood studio media conglomerates. A studio-related entity was involved in the funding of production, via the purchase of distribution rights, even if it was not the first on board; but it was only one of several initial backers. The fact that Focus International did not have a single, controlling influence might be more important

in making a case *for* independent industrial status than its presence in
any form is in arguing *against*, although what this really demonstrates
most clearly is how inexact any such definitions are or have become in
recent decades. Industrially, as in other respects, 'independent' is a relative rather than an absolute or clear-cut category, as I have argued at
length elsewhere.[10] The practice of funding production initially by the
sale of overseas rights to different players in different territories certainly
seemed to attract positive treatment for *Lost in Translation* in some influential indie-oriented quarters, including the pages of *Filmmaker* magazine
(published by the Independent Feature Project, a membership-based
organisation that provides support and advocacy for the sector), whose
correspondent refers to the film being financed 'Jim Jarmusch-style',
the evocation of a name strongly associated with what might be understood to be 'core' indie values.[11] (Jarmusch, whose films have often been
funded by advance deals with territories including Europe and Japan,
subsequently appeared to return the compliment by casting Murray
somewhat similarly as star of his next project, *Broken Flowers* [2005].) With
its initial investors on board, the production secured additional finance
from the French bank Natexis Banques Populaires, another overseas
source that contributed to the general impression of proximity to indie/
alternative rather than studio financial strategy.

Pre-production began, however, before the complete package was in
place and while the status of the film remained uncertain. Tohokushinsha
funded initial costs of $1 million, permitting the project to get off the
ground in Tokyo, before anyone was entirely sure whether Murray
would turn up for the shoot, an act of faith that ensured that the various
elements of the production could be held together in the period before
the star's presence would be required on set. 'It was nerve-wracking',
Coppola was quoted as observing, before Murray arrived a week before
the start of shooting and the future of the film was ensured.[12] The shoot
itself had more in common with indie than usual studio practice, adopting an approach described variously as 'guerrilla style', 'run and gun',
'Dogme-style' and 'almost documentary-style for some scenes', the latter
being Coppola's own phrase.[13] Coppola arrived in Tokyo with much of
the look and feel of the film already established in her head, according to
her producer, Ross Katz, although the sparse nature of the script permit-
ted a good deal of scope for improvisation of both shooting and dialogue
on set or location.[14]

The schedule was a very tight twenty-seven days and required shooting

Figure 2 'Guerrilla-style': director of photography Lance Acord shooting hand-held on the streets of Tokyo. © 2003 Universal Studios

by both day and night. The central location was the luxury Park Hyatt hotel, a familiar venue to the writer-director from previous visits to the city. To avoid disruption to guests, shooting at the hotel had to be completed at night. It was out on the streets, key sources of some of the distinctive atmospherics of the film, that the guerrilla/Dogme/documentary-style was most evidently employed. Sequences of this kind were shot in an impromptu manner with a small crew and hand-held camera, without any crowd control or official permissions, in locations such as busy streets and the Tokyo subway. The director of photography, Lance Acord, employed a lightweight Aaton camera and film stock of higher-than-usual speed, to reduce the need for lighting. The aim was to shoot in a flexible, mobile style that was both a practicality for a low-budget production and a central contribution to the fleeting impression created of the texture of the city, very different from the usual studio procedure in which streets would be closed off, a range of permits would be required and the whole process would be far more controlled and expensive.[15] Coppola was reported to have resisted budgetary pressure to shoot on digital video, a form well-suited to such an approach, seeking to combine immediacy of access to real locations with the more romantic and distanced impression associated with the industry-standard 35mm film (for a closer examination of the aesthetics that resulted, see Chapter 3).[16] Acord offered assurances that newly available stocks 'were flexible enough to prevent the lighting budget from becoming an issue'.[17] The stock employed for exteriors (Kodak's Vision 500T 5263) had what he described as 'a soft, slightly desaturated feel that subtly enhanced the otherworldly feel that Tokyo naturally exudes.' In addition to the principal photography, second-unit footage of the city was shot by Coppola's older brother, Roman. Considerable scope for improvisation was given to the central performers, especially drawing on the comic talents of Murray, who arrived too late to allow much opportunity for rehearsal. This, along with the strategy of 'shooting on the fly', was cited by *Variety* as one of the dimensions of the film that would have given a studio 'several cases of the heebie-jeebies' if it had been in control of the production.[18] One scene that was almost entirely improvised features the central characters singing karaoke, shot before potentially expensive permissions were gained for the use of any of the songs, including Murray's strained rendition of 'More than This' by Roxy Music (for which clearance was, eventually, obtained).

A further respect in which the fictional events of the film mirrored aspects of the reality experienced by the writer-director resulted from the use of a largely Japanese crew, another budgetary necessity. A number of key personnel were American, including former Coppola collaborators Acord and the costume designer, Nancy Steiner, but much of what was to be conveyed to other crew members had to be translated into Japanese, through a bilingual assistant director. The result was an effect similar to that dramatised in the comic sequences in *Lost in Translation* in which Bill Murray's character takes direction through an intermediary during the shooting of his Suntory endorsements. In some cases, it seems, confusion and misunderstanding resulted on set, which slowed down the pace of proceedings. In one instance this led to a cross-cultural misunderstanding that resulted in the resignation of the Japanese location manager, deemed to have lost face when the production over-ran its agreed time limits while shooting in a restaurant location.[19] Some members of cast and crew, including Murray, also suffered from jet-lag, another reality of the production that figures centrally in the diegesis.[20] The first, rough, assembly of the film was created from videotape dailies posted from Japan to editor Sarah Flack, followed by some ten weeks of editing overseen by Coppola in New York.[21]

Distribution, marketing and release: The pull of Indiewood

Once production and post-production were complete, a key indicator of the industrial status of *Lost in Translation* was the choice of a US domestic distributor (assuming a choice to be available, as opposed to the situation faced by many independent films of having to take anything they can get). It is at this point that the film moved more firmly into the Indiewood realm, and where the existing involvement of Focus International proved decisive. US rights were obtained by Focus Features, a quintessentially Indiewood institution, the domestic theatrical 'speciality' division of the NBC Universal media empire, which gained a significant advantage through the prior investment made by its overseas arm. Coppola's final cut of *Lost in Translation* was screened on video projection for Focus heads James Schamus and David Linde. Other distributors, meanwhile, were restricted to a three-minute trailer shown in the Focus offices at the American Film Market (AFM), a major event in the film sales calendar, in February 2003. The advertised price was $5 million, but the rights were sold to Focus at the AFM for $4 million, a cut reported by *Variety* to have been Coppola's mark of gratitude for the deals the company's international wing had made for the film overseas.[22] The connection between Coppola, Schamus and Linde had, in fact, preceded the creation of Focus, dating back to the role of the two executives at the head of Good Machine, a noted part of the New York independent scene, which was absorbed into the studio division in 2002; the international arm of Good Machine became the basis of Focus International. Coppola was a filmmaker 'we really wanted to be in business with' after impressing the company with *The Virgin Suicides*, according to Linde, and had discussed the sale of the international rights to *Lost in Translation* with Good Machine just before the latter was sold to Universal. Once the film had gone into production with the support of Focus International, Linde says, 'we just kept trying to attract her to work with us domestically, as well.'[23]

The competition was reported to have been unhappy at the inside track and favourable treatment gained by Focus, a process that underlines the importance for indie/speciality distributors of gaining an early stake in what might be expected to be the more commercially attractive projects. Through the involvement of its international division, Focus gained something close to a first-look option on the film, a practice commonly used by the studios to secure priority access to product, although usually the subject of more formal agreement. The initial role played by Focus International can be understood in hindsight, therefore, to have pulled the production closer to the Indiewood arena than might originally have appeared to be the case. For those suspicious of any such involvement of entities tied to the major studios, it can be seen to have performed as a Trojan horse for the domestic activities of the speciality division. The arrangement appears to have been very much a mutual one for filmmaker and distributor, however. The early presence of Focus International was clearly an important part of the initial funding/ rights package, from the perspective of Coppola, as a writer-director seeking freedom at the production stage. It also gave Focus Features privileged access to a project that fitted very well into the particular niche it was seeking to carve in the indie or more broadly defined 'speciality' market.

Focus Features was the latest in a number of entities created or bought by Universal in order to service the indie/speciality sector, part of a broader movement towards studio investment in this part of the cinematic spectrum.[24] This phase of the process was begun for Universal in 1997 with the purchase of the noted indie distributor October Films. Universal was also involved in Gramercy Films, another significant name in the breakthrough period of indie cinema from the late 1980s, as a joint venture with PolyGram Filmed Entertainment (a subsidiary of the Dutch electronics company, Philips). Gramercy and October subsequently became part of USA Films, a division of the former studio head Barry Diller's USA Networks, returning to the Universal fold when USA Networks was merged with the studio's then corporate parent, Vivendi. In the meantime, Universal Focus was created as a new speciality entity. It was rebranded as Focus Features after Universal bought Good Machine, folding it and USA Films into the new-look division. The resulting creation had a strong indie pedigree, particularly in the presence at its head of Schamus and Linde, two of the three former partners in Good Machine, which had established its status as one of the leading lights in the New York indie scene from the 1990s.

For the studio/corporate owners of Focus, Schamus and Linde brought knowledge and experience of the speciality market and ongoing relationships with a number of filmmakers who had established prominence in the sector. In this and other respects, Universal was following what had, by the early 2000s, become a familiar model. The success of a number of indie features from the late 1980s and into the 1990s prompted all of the Hollywood studios to invest in the sector in one way or another, either by establishing their own divisions to handle indie/specialist films (including some overseas imports) or taking over independent distributors and/or producers. A precursor to this phenomenon was the creation of short-lived 'classics' divisions during the 1980s, a development that included Universal alongside United Artists and 20th Century Fox. The 1990s saw a more concerted process of studio involvement in the indie realm, a key difference of which was that a greater degree of autonomy was given to speciality divisions, to take advantage of the kind of expertise possessed by figures such as Schamus and Linde. Thus Harvey and Bob Weinstein were retained at the head of Miramax, the biggest and most influential player in the 1990s independent sector, when it was sold to Disney in 1993, as was Bob Shaye when New Line became part of Time-Warner via its sale to Ted Turner.[25] Other studio divisions created during the 1990s included Sony Pictures Classics (1992), Fox Searchlight (1994) and Paramount Classics (1998, later renamed Paramount Vantage), followed by Warner Independent Pictures in 2003 (the Warner division was subsequently closed as part of restructuring in 2008).

Focus enjoyed considerable success from the start, its first acquisition, *The Pianist* (2002), winning three Academy Awards, including best director for Roman Polanski. *Lost in Translation* was to prove its most successful and prominent offering of 2003 and became something of a talisman for the company, one of the films singled out to signify the particular qualities it sought to associate with the Focus brand, as will be seen below. Its treatment immediately before and during its domestic opening was a demonstration of typical Indiewood strategy, combining a number of more traditionally indie dimensions with a release that crossed over into broader theatrical territory. The advance marketing strategy included preview screenings designed to create positive word-of-mouth reaction during the summer of 2003, well ahead of the release in mid-September. This was combined with advance publicity that included a highly favourable portrait of Coppola and the film in a front-cover feature in the *New York Times* magazine.[26] The film was also placed in high-status film festivals immediately prior to release, premiering at Telluride in Colorado, a prestige event in the American festival circuit, followed shortly afterwards by an appearance at the Venice Film Festival, which brought association with the qualities of international art cinema (it also picked up two of the more minor awards at Venice, for Coppola and Johansson). What were described as 'intimate' media screenings were also arranged, including question-and-answer sessions with Coppola and Murray, the latter likely to attract particular attention given the often reclusive nature of the performer.[27] In combination, this is a familiar indie-style recipe, seeking to create and maximise positive word for a film at relatively minimal cost, especially when compared with the huge spending on television and other marketing associated with the contemporary Hollywood mainstream. Features such as the cover story in the *New York Times* magazine, the tone of which *Variety* described as 'rapturous', are particularly valued, offering unpaid-for publicity of a kind that could not be bought. As the *Variety* correspondent put it: 'It mentioned the film in the same breath as "Academy Award" within the second paragraph and compared the director to Chekhov in the third', an ideal combination of reference points suggesting both popular and more elevated forms of prestige. That *Lost in Translation* was likely awards material, particularly in the run-up to the Oscars that begins in the autumn of each year, soon became an established part of critical and other media discourse surrounding the film and the way it was positioned in the wider cultural marketplace.

The release itself started on a typically indie scale, although one that soon expanded more widely. *Lost in Translation* opened on 14 September 2003, on twenty-three screens in New York, Los Angeles and San Francisco. The focus in the first week was clearly at the upmarket, metro-politan end of the scale, seeking viewers in large, culturally 'sophisticated' urban areas, very much in tune with the indie model established in the 1980s and 1990s. The choice of date was less conventional, however, some weeks earlier than what had become recognised as the standard award-contending indie, speciality or 'prestige' release window of later autumn. The trade press noted the strategy, described in *Variety* as 'a bold distribution move', another manner in which the film sought to get ahead of the likely opposition in staking its claim to the status of major awards contender and most high-profile indie or prestige picture of the upcoming season.[28] According to Jack Foley, head of distribution, Focus decided 'to break out of the usual assumption and be much more aggres-sive about planting the flag earlier in the fall', on the basis of the film's festival exposure 'and the extraordinarily enthusiastic response we know the film would get from real cinephiles.' An additional factor cited by Foley was the 'rather clear playing field' gained by the film as a result, which would give audiences more space to discover it for themselves in the face of less competition from similarly pitched productions (with the help, of course, of the marketing campaign, more of which is considered below).[29]

In a sense, what Focus was seeking to create in a rather different context was a situation similar to that achieved by some productions in the realm of the Hollywood blockbuster in previous decades, a process in which the peak season for a particular type of product was pushed back earlier in the calendar (in that case, back to early or pre-summer, in May, rather than peak summer) in order to lengthen the period in which an individual film – or slate including a succession of blockbuster-scale productions – might dominate the market. It is not clear that the Focus strategy in the case of *Lost in Translation* has been more widely adopted in the indie and/or Indiewood sectors, although this is a region of the marketplace in which distributors have tended to experiment on occasion with less conventional openings (not least Focus in the case of one of its trademark features of the following year, *Eternal Sunshine of the Spotless Mind* [2004], which was released in March on a much more substantial 1,353 screens, a strategy based to a large extent on the presence of Jim Carrey as a star with greater crossover potential[30]). The potential risk in going so early would be that, if less successful, a film might be lost from the necessary consciousness too soon to be best positioned for inclusion among leading Oscar and other major awards contenders.

For critics of Indiewood who see the cooptation of elements of the independent sector by Hollywood as a threat to productions that remain more distanced from the studios, the Focus strategy of opening *Lost in Translation* earlier than would usually be expected might be interpreted as a kind of bullying by the more powerful players (an impression that might be supported by the language of being 'aggressive' and the military metaphor of 'planting the flag' employed by Foley). Foley himself commented in 2004 on the negative impact the release had on rivals in what he termed the 'smart market', suggesting that it had 'a crippling effect on those in the high-end market' that had opened either shortly before Coppola's film, in August (a less conventional slot when they would also face competition from late-summer high-budget studio fare), or after it, in the prime later-autumn window. This was an acknowledgement of what Foley termed the 'fragility' of the market, the fact that one dominant speciality/prestige film could overwhelm others in this part of the commercial landscape.[31] Another potential advantage for Focus in opening the film earlier than usual, and thereby extending the autumn window, was to spread the release of its own most high-profile films of the season. It cleared space for a gap between *Lost in Translation* and successors such as *Sylvia* (19 October opening) and *21 Grams* (23 November), thus reducing the risk of its films competing too closely against one another, a familiar problem in the often crowded independent or Indiewood sectors.

As far as opposition in the all-important week of release was concerned, the moment of key visibility and media attention, *Lost in Translation* faced little direct competition in its particular market niche. The biggest releases of the weekend, just after the end of the extended summer block-buster season on which Hollywood depends for a disproportionate share of its theatrical revenue, were relatively modest but firmly mainstream productions, as would be expected: Robert Rodriguez' *Once Upon a Time in Mexico*, an 'epic' $29 million action sequel to his previously break-through ultra-low-budget indie hit, *El Mariachi* (1992), on 3,282 screens, and *Matchstick Men*, a Warner-released con-artist picture directed by Ridley Scott and starring Nicolas Cage and Sam Rockwell, on 2,711 screens. Below these, from the horror/exploitation end of the independent sector, came *Cabin Fever*, released on 2,087 screens by the largest non-studio-affiliated US distributor, Lions Gate.[32] The next biggest release was the thriller *No Good Deed* (aka *The House on Turk Street*), starring Samuel L. Jackson, on 402 screens. Of the films on more restricted release, none was in a territory very close to that occupied by *Lost in Translation*. The Hong Kong action film *So Close* (*Chik Yeung tin sai*), was on eleven screens; the Japanese import *Millennium Actress* (*Sennen joyûi)* on six; the indie romantic comedy *Dummy* on five; the German documentary about a human rights activist, *Warrior of Light* (*Kriegerin des Lichts*), and the gay-oriented *Luster* on one apiece.

The closest of these offerings to *Lost in Translation*, in broad terms, was *Dummy*, an independent production released through Artisan Entertainment, a substantial indie distributor that was taken over by Lions Gate three months later. *Dummy* is in several respects a typical, perhaps routine, indie comedy/drama/romance featuring a 'loveable loser', surrounded by a mostly eccentric supporting cast, who dreams of becoming a ventriloquist. It grossed $30,120 on its opening weekend, a per-screen average of a fraction over $6,000. If it was competing for some of the same territory as *Lost in Translation*, it clearly lost out heavily. The latter took a total of $925,087, achieving what the online indie newsletter *indieWIRE* described as a 'huge' screen average of $40,221, 'the highest for the specialty box office in 2003'.[33] For Jack Foley, quoted at the time, the average 'sets a new standard'. Responses in exit surveys conducted for Focus were very positive and word of mouth was strong, according to Foley, who added that returns for the film had been 'remarkable' in dropping little from Saturday to Sunday screenings, in some cases rising, which he declared to be 'extremely rare'.[34] On the basis of these figures, the film was spread significantly wider in its second week, to 183 screens in the top twenty-five markets across the country, grossing $2.62 million over the weekend with a screen average that was smaller but still described by *indieWIRE* as 'tsunami-sized' at $14,332.[35] Week three saw further expansion, to 488 screens in fifty or more markets, and a weekend gross of $3.68 million and a still strong average of $7,558. The following week it spread wider still, to 864 screens, grossing $4.16 million for the weekend at an average of $4,818. A slightly higher number of screens was reached in the fifth week, the film's peak of 882 (weekend gross, $3.16 million; average $3,588). The pattern was one of substantial but measured expansion, followed by a gradual decline that sustained the film as a solid substantial-niche performer into the New Year – after which it gained a renewed boost during the major awards season, as detailed below.

Dummy, meanwhile, very soon disappeared from view. Its five-screen release was maintained for the second weekend, with returns dropping to $17,803. By the third week it was down to two screens (weekend gross: $2,990) and it ended its run in the fourth on a single screen, taking $1,219 for the weekend and a very modest overall US gross of $71,305 (for one other measure of comparison, *Lost in Translation* only reached a screen average as low as that experienced by the final weekend of *Dummy* in March 2004, its 27th week in theatres, although it also dipped below $1,500 in mid-December).[36] Whether or not it would have done better, or lasted longer, without the presence of *Lost in Translation* is impossible to determine but the space available to such productions is related quite directly to the nature of the immediate competition; not just physical space on screens, which is always in short supply for indie features under pressure to perform quickly or be pulled from release, but also space for the kind of media and broader word-of-mouth attention on the basis of which Coppola's film appeared to thrive.

Lost in Translation seemed to benefit from strong word-of-mouth recommendation beyond what might have been expected to be its core audience. According to *The Hollywood Reporter*, four weeks into the release:

It's not just working in New York and L.A. and other big cities where you'd expect it to perform well, but it's also generating big grosses in smaller or medium sized markets where audiences don't always respond to this type of upscale material.[37]

The report goes on to quote David Linde:

In this day and age even in small markets like Louisville, Kentucky, it's playing in an eight-screen theater . . . Or in Plano, Texas it's in, whatever, a 16-screen theater. It's not only holding up to its sort of 'traditional specialized audience', but it's holding up really in the theaters against fierce competition.

Weekly figures were cited in the same article by James Schamus:

'From Monday to Monday', Schamus said, 'it went up in just about every marketplace in the country. In Phoenix, it went up 139%. It Hartford it went up 66%. In Miami-Ft. Lauderdale in its fourth week in that city, (it went up) 22% from Monday to Monday. So the word of mouth is really good on the movie. Birmingham, Alabama (was up) 163%. Providence, Rhode Island (was up) 125%. It's really amazing.'[38]

This suggests the achievement of a significant degree of cross-over success. As far as non-specialised alternatives were concerned, *Lost in Translation* was competing in the general market with a number of mainstream features, although none that might be expected totally to dominate the scene. In addition to *Once Upon a Time in Mexico*, *Matchstick Men* and *Cabin Fever*, these included the later stages of the long run of the summer blockbuster *Pirates of the Caribbean: The Curse of the Black Pearl* and new releases in its second week such as *Underworld* (action/vampires), *Secondhand Lions* (family-oriented comedy) and the gospel-choir-oriented comedy *The Fighting Temptations*. In its third week, the box office was led by *The Rundown* (action-adventure starring The Rock) and the emotional comedy-drama *Under the Tuscan Sun*, closely followed by two of the new releases of the previous weekend. The top films in the fourth week of the run were Richard Linklater's comedy *School of Rock* and the suspense thriller *Out of Time*, starring Denzel Washington. All of these films outperformed *Lost in Translation* several-fold as far as box-office gross was concerned, the biggest openings belonging to *Underworld* ($21,753,759),

School of Rock ($19,622,714) and *The Rundown* ($18,533,765), in week-ends during which Coppola's film grossed $2,622,737, $4,163,333 and $3,695,901 respectively.[39] In its first four weeks, *Lost in Translation* was placed 15th, 10th, 10th and 7th in the *Variety* box office chart, the latter being the highest point it was to reach.

Released at a time generally viewed as an interregnum for the studios, as far as their most commercially important blockbuster-scale produc-tions are concerned, between the summer and Christmas holiday peak seasons, *Lost in Translation* appeared a modest box-office performer by Hollywood standards, even though it was considered a great success in indie or Indiewood terms. Its final domestic theatrical gross was $44,566,004, a relatively modest sum in itself but not when compared with a budget of just $4 million: an eleven-fold return (minus the costs of release and marketing) before overseas and video/DVD revenues are included, the latter usually considerably out-performing theatrical returns (overseas box-office was put at $75,138,403, giving a total theat-rical revenue of more than $119 million.[40] The cost/revenue comparison with the larger-grossing films in its first four weeks of release is striking. *Underworld* grossed a total of $51,970,690, more than *Lost in Translation*, but on a much higher budget, estimated at $22 million. *School of Rock* returned $81,257,845 in the US, but on a budget put at $35 million, a broadly similar ratio. *The Rundown* took $47,592,825, a little more than *Lost in Translation*, but this represented a considerable loss in the first instance for a production budgeted at $85 million.[41] These figures certainly demonstrate the commercial appeal of titles such as *Lost in Translation*, as part of the broader slates of studios and their speciality divi-sions. They can be highly profitable on their own terms, even if the total sums involved are substantially smaller than those earned by successful holiday blockbusters.

Lost in Translation was established early as a likely awards contender, as suggested in the *New York Times* magazine article cited above, a significant ingredient in its ability to be positioned as a 'quality', 'prestige' produc-tion and at the same time to reach out to more than a narrow niche audience. The film approached the all-important nominations for the Academy Awards in a strong position, having been nominated for five Golden Globes, awarded by the Hollywood Foreign Press Association, a traditional forerunner to the Oscars. It won three Globes ('Best Motion Picture – Musical or Comedy', best actor in a musical or comedy for Bill Murray and best screenplay) among other prestigious pre-Oscar awards including 'Outstanding Directorial Achievement in Motion Pictures' for Coppola from the Director's Guild of America. It was reported, at this stage, to have been named best film of the year by more than 235 critics.[42] *Lost in Translation* received Oscar nominations for best film, best director, best actor and best original screenplay, going on to win in the latter category. The importance of the Academy Award season for such films was marked by an expansion of its release, which had declined during November and December. January saw the number of sites in which it was playing increase from a low of 117 at the end of December to 342 on 11 January and slightly higher (366 and 357) on the next two weekends, immediately before the publication of nominations, and to 632, 630 and 600 in the three weeks that followed, with a boost also to its per-screen average.[43] Approximately $12 million of the $44 million grossed by the film was taken in this period, a significant boost towards the end of its run and one of the major reasons for the attraction of studio divisions to Oscar-potential projects of this kind. Oscar-related publicity would also be expected to impact very positively on overseas revenues. There was little expectation that *Lost in Translation* would be serious competition for best film, an award widely predicted to go to *Lord of the Rings: The Return of the King*, but it was considered by the trade press to have performed strongly by gaining four top nominations. As one of the five nominees for best film it took what *The Hollywood Reporter* termed 'the Academy's unofficial slot as the year's best independent film'.[44]

If the expansion of the release during Oscar season was conventional practice, taking advantage of the burst of publicity that could be expected to result from nominations as much as awards, Focus moved into relatively uncharted waters by also releasing *Lost in Translation* on DVD at the time, before the end of its theatrical run. In this respect, the performance of the film was viewed as a test of an issue of wider concern to both Hollywood and independent distributors: exactly what the relationship should be between theatrical and home-view release, and how close together the two could occur without damage to one or the other (a prevailing industry concern, not least among exhibitors, being that early DVD release could be harmful to theatrical business, prompting many prospective viewers to stay at home rather than venturing out to a cinema). Hollywood studios had, in the previous years, tended to reduce the gap between these two most important windows, partly to limit the impact of piracy and – probably more significantly – to gain earlier access to the home-viewing revenues that tend to provide the lion's share of income. The issue also had a particular currency in the independent sector, where simultaneous theatrical/DVD release has been considered a potentially more effective way of responding to a situation in which the theatrical audience for smaller films – located only in select metropolitan areas – is rarely commensurate with the costs of the promotion required to make such viewers aware of their existence.[45]

Viewers appeared to be happy to have the choice, as far as *Lost in Translation* was concerned. The DVD, released immediately after the announcement of the Oscar nominations, sold what was considered to be a very healthy one million retail copies in its first week, in mid-February, and earned nearly $5 million in rental revenue in its first five days of release, while the film was showing on 600 screens. Box-office declined by what *Variety* termed only 'a relatively modest' 19 per cent from the previous week.[46] Whether or not this was a special case remained open to debate, with the emphasis from Focus executives put on the particular status of the film. For Jack Foley, 'we believe that the phenomenon of "Lost in Translation" succeeding in both mediums is unique and indicative of the incredible support for this special film.'[47] It is likely to have benefited from marketing synergy across the two formats, as suggested by the parent company Universal's head of home video, Craig Kornblau, who hedged his bets on whether or not *Lost in Translation* was likely to be a one-off on the basis of its 'tremendous word of mouth'.[48]

If its Academy Award nominations and success gave *Lost in Translation* mainstream recognition and a boost in both box-office and DVD sales, it also gained indie credibility by winning in several of the major categories of the Independent Spirit Awards, organised by the Independent Feature Project, on the eve of the Oscar ceremony. Its presence at the two events, in such close proximity, was further evidence of its hybrid nature as a film with feet in both the studio-oriented and more indie-distinctive camps. In the Spirit awards, *Lost in Translation* triumphed with best feature, best director, best screenplay and best male lead, making it the clear overall winner on the day. The greater scale of its success in the IFP awards might be taken as an indicator of the fact that the film skews to the indie side several degrees more than to the mainstream, although its place in the Academy Awards was of far greater cultural prominence and commercial significance. Whether such films should figure in the Spirit awards is an ongoing matter of dispute, the inclusion of Indiewood or borderline indie/Indiewood productions such as *Lost in Translation* frequently being criticised by figures within the independent movement

Figure 3 Selling the character-star presence: the narrative frame imposed in the trailer. © 2003 Universal Studios

for taking up a space that should be devoted to more distinctively and otherwise less advantaged indie productions, one of the purposes of the awards being to create a showcase for material less likely to figure in its mainstream equivalents. In 2004, the film was joined in facing such criticism by Jim Sheridan's *In America*, a Fox Searchlight release.[49] One of *Lost in Translation*'s key claims to belong in this arena was its budgetary scale (along with the method of financing production detailed above), a ground on which one of Focus's other key releases of the year, *21 Grams*, was disqualified from the main awards (although so confused is this territory that *21 Grams* was given a Special Distinction award, which suggested that the organisers wanted to include it in some form despite its $20–22 million budget[50]).

From pre-publicity to theatrical opening, expansion, awards success and DVD release, *Lost in Translation* appeared to be a model of how successfully to orchestrate the career of a film in a manner that draws on elements of established indie/niche and more aggressive/broader Indiewood strategies. Something similar can be said of the manner in which the film was marketed in posters and trailers, and subsequently employed as one of the components in what was meant to be signified by the Focus brand. Primary position in the main posters and trailers is given to Bill Murray as the central star presence. The main US trailer begins by presenting a narrative about Murray's character, Bob, interspersed in lines of text between scenes from the film. The narrative line runs as follows: 'Bob Is An Actor', 'Bob Is Lost', 'Bob Doesn't Speak The Language', 'Fortunately For Bob' 'Friendship Needs No Translation'. After text crediting Coppola as 'writer and director' and name-checks for Murray and Johansson, the narrative headings conclude: 'Sometimes You Have to Go Halfway Around The World', 'To Come Full Circle'. The choice of extracts from the film is telling, the trailer being dominated by sequences that emphasise the comic dimension of the production and particularly Murray's performance. The early stages include footage from Bob's whisky advertisement shoot, with its language gaps played for deadpan comedy; his appearance with an over-the-top TV-show host; his display of 'rat pack' poses during a still photography session; and part of a bizarre scene in which a woman visits his hotel room asking him to 'lip' (i.e. 'rip') her stocking (one of a number of not very subtle jokes in the film at the expense of Japanese pronunciation of English, an issue to which we return later). At the point of 'Fortunately For Bob', Charlotte is brought into the picture and the central relationship is briefly sketched, along with her suggestion that he is undergoing a 'mid-life crisis'.

Further comic scenes are cut into this material, including Bob on an out-of-control exercise machine, singing karaoke, and briefly wrestling with a too-low shower head. The latter stages of the trailer go some way towards evoking the film's broader take on relationships, particularly in the final two headings, as does some of the background imagery of Tokyo and some of the dialogue fragments exchanged between the principals. A disproportionate amount of comic footage is included, however, elements of most of the instances of broader comedy and/or comic performance in the film. This seems to be a clear favouring of what would be expected to be the dimension of the film most likely to appeal to a wider audience. Murray is not named up-front, but would be expected to be recognisable to many viewers, and his comic performance – both in the film and in frames-within-the-frame, as an actor playing an actor – is heavily foregrounded. A romantic dimension might be implied, with the introduction of Charlotte, but it is also notable, on the more distinctive/ indie side of the equation, that the term used in the titles is 'friendship', as opposed to anything more romantically or sexually oriented, as might be expected in a more conventional production (issues the substance of which are considered in Chapters 2 and 3).

The overall impression created by the trailer is somewhat mixed, including intimations of a general hesitancy or uncertainty in the tone of some of the dialogue, as befits the nature of the film, but it is unsurprising that the most obvious commercial hook – Murray himself or the more compound quality of Murray-in-comic-performance – is by far the strongest single point of emphasis. Murray's figure also dominated poster and DVD cover artwork. The main poster, used as the basis of DVD covers, features Murray sitting on the side of his hotel-room bed. His face bears a bemused expression and he is dressed in slippers and a bath-robe that leaves his knees exposed, garb that contributes to a generally deadpan comic impression. Above the title, towards the top of the image, Murray and Johansson's names are given equal-sized billing. The tagline reads 'Everyone wants to be found', implying, it seems, the likelihood of a romance. An alternative poster features Johansson's face towards the edge of the frame, much of the space being devoted to Tokyo background neon and the figure of a dinosaur on a giant advertising wall-screen, a version the primary resonances of which are very different and less clear-cut. The DVD covers stuck with the Murray version, with the addition of indications of the film's positive critical reputation. A strip across the top of the region 1 (US and Canada) release depicts four large stars and the legend: 'OVER 80 FOUR-STAR RAVE REVIEWS!', along with a quotation from *US Weekly* reading: 'GETTING LOST NEVER FELT SO GOOD!" The region 2 (Europe etc.) release followed suit in its textual emphasis on reviews, quoting from four of them: 'PHENOMENAL . . . FILM OF THE YEAR!'; 'Hysterically FUNNY'; 'A TRIUMPH!'; and 'Bill Murray is MAGNIFICENT'.

The emphasis on positive reviews is consistent with an indie approach, critical approval generally being considered more important in the speciality than the mainstream market. The use of such quotations in the particular context of cover or poster artwork is also widespread in many Hollywood features, however. In content, the extracts selected lean primarily towards the promise of mainstream cinematic pleasures. Terms such as 'phenomenal', 'film of the year' and 'a triumph' might also be applicable to products from the less commercial end of the spectrum, but to a reduced extent when combined with the likes of 'never felt so good', 'hysterically funny' and an emphasis on the 'magnificence' of Bill Murray, phrasings that suggest an appeal to the dynamics of mainstream popular entertainment rather than selling more distinctive qualities in the film to those who might position themselves as more 'discerning'. Sofia Coppola's name appears on the main poster and the DVD covers, but in a marginal position. The poster describes *Lost in Translation* as 'The new film written and directed by Sofia Coppola', which is quite strong and slightly unusual phrasing ('The new film', rather than just 'written and directed by' or 'by'), but positioned at the very bottom edge, below the main credit block. On the DVD the more conventional 'Written and directed by Sofia Coppola' appears in relatively small type below the title, further suggesting (along with no more than a passing mention in the middle of the trailer) that the identity of the filmmaker is not being used to any great extent in the selling of the film through these media. As far as these forms of marketing are concerned, *Lost in Translation* is a Bill Murray film more than anything else, a dimension examined in more detail in the following chapter.

The presence of Murray also figures centrally in the manner in which *Lost in Translation* was used by Focus as one of its trademark features in promotional materials designed to sell the distinctive nature of the studio division's own brand. The region 1 DVD release is accompanied by what amounts to a show-reel, a composite trailer that places the film alongside *The Pianist* (2002), *Far from Heaven* (2002), *The Kid Stays in the Picture* (2002), *Eternal Sunshine of the Spotless Mind*, *Monsoon Wedding* (2002) and *Gosford Park* (2001, distributed by USA Films before the creation of Focus Features). The accompanying voice-over declares a company mission to make 'superior quality films that are as rich and distinct as the world around us, that defy conventions and dare to be extraordinary.' That, it continues, is why 'we've become *the* destination for the world's biggest movie stars and most acclaimed filmmakers, a home for their most personal and passionate projects.' The emphasis on 'superior quality', richness, distinctiveness and personal/passionate projects is balanced by reference to the more mainstream marketability of stars. In the roll-call of films that follows the initial commentary, each title is accompanied by 'starring' or 'with' and the names of Murray and Johansson; Sean Penn, Benicio Del Toro and Naomi Watts (*21 Grams*); 'Academy Award winner Gwyneth Paltrow' (*Sylvia*); Heath Ledger, Orlando Bloom, Naomi Watts and Geoffrey Rush (*Ned Kelly*); Jim Carrey, Kate Winslet and Kirsten Dunst (*Eternal Sunshine of the Spotless Mind*); Jeff Bridges and Kim Basinger (*The Door in the Floor*); Reese Witherspoon (*Vanity Fair*). The blend of 'quality' and star names appears typically Indiewood in character, as do the choice of dramatic or eye-catching image fragments and dialogue extracts that accompany the voice-over.[51] A similar positioning of the company's releases is found in the 'Focus Reel' supplied on its website, in which a clip from *Lost in Translation* was accompanied at the time by the one-word claim 'Original'.[52]

Murray was a key source of orientation in reviews from major US critics, whose overwhelmingly positive general response played an important part in the spread of the good word-of-mouth that was credited with driving the film to its success at the box office. The emphasis in reviews was distributed more widely, however, with Coppola more closely rivalling her star for attention than is the case in posters, DVD covers or the trailer. Greater emphasis on the filmmaker – as a distinctive auteur presence or more generally – would usually be expected to be found at the 'higher' or 'quality' end of the press spectrum, although this is only partially the case for *Lost in Translation*. The newspaper reviews generally accorded greatest importance and influence for films of this kind – productions for which positive review coverage is generally considered to be more than averagely important – are those appearing in *The New York Times* and the *Los Angeles Times*, key initial reference points in the east- and west-coast markets. In terms of who gets first treatment in their reviews, they split evenly between Coppola and Murray. The *New York Times* review begins: 'The director Sofia Coppola's new comic melodrama', going on to situate the film in relation to three others and mentioning its comic qualities, citing Murray directly only in the third paragraph, although the text that follows devotes close attention to his performance.[53] The *Los Angeles Times* opens with direct reference to the star: 'Statistics are hard to come by, but citizens hungering for meatier roles for Bill Murray could be the largest unorganized group of moviegoers in the country.'[54] Johansson is cited next, in the second paragraph, followed by Coppola, 'a mature talent with a distinctive sensibility and the means to express it.' The bodies of the two reviews pay due heed to each, although with Murray generally closer to the centre of attention.

In more popular publications, the emphasis would conventionally be expected quite strongly to favour the star, as a point of reference likely to be more familiar to the majority of readers, although the picture with *Lost in Translation* is, again, rather more mixed than that would suggest. The tabloid *New York Post* puts Coppola's name first in its review ('Sofia Coppola's sublimely romantic and subtle "Lost in Translation" finally marks the end of a season of brain-dead blockbusters.').[55] Murray is left to the second paragraph, where he gets a strongly positive response, while the remainder of the review mixes recounting of plot with interspersed comments primarily relating to star and filmmaker. *USA Today* opens with Murray's name and gives him pride of place overall, although Coppola is given substantially more than passing attention, cited in the second sentence, again in the second paragraph, approvingly, and towards the end.[56] One of the generally more high-profile and substantial online review sources, Salon.com, also offers a broadly equal blend of attention at the start, although favouring Coppola overall.[57] Her name forms the opening words ('Sofia Coppola's magnificent and delicate') and is a close point of reference throughout, in a review that has high praise for Murray's performance but that devotes sustained attention to creating an impression of a number of qualities attributed to the writer-director. Citations of Coppola and Murray in all of these reviews include either explicit or implicit attention to the more distinctive/indie dimensions of the film, an obvious example being the comparison with 'brain-dead blockbusters' in the *New York Post*.

The wider press reception of *Lost in Translation* was highly favourable, most reviewers broadly following the lead established by the major US critics. Ninety-five per cent of 205 reviews surveyed by the Rotten Tomatoes website were judged to be positive (194 being placed in the highest category, 'fresh', and only eleven categorised as 'rotten', giving an average rating of 8.4 out of 10.[58] A similar finding is offered by Metacritic, a rating of 89 out of 100 on the basis of a weighted analysis of forty-four published reviews.[59] Responses to the film posted on viewer-oriented websites are strongly polarised, however, demonstrating far less of a consensus than that found in the work of most professional critics and highlighting the more particular and partial nature of the kinds of qualities that tend to be the main bases of appeal to the latter. A snapshot of this difference is visible in the ratings provided by Metacritic, in the comparison between the rating attributed to critics and the more modest average score of 6.3 out of 10 provided by votes from 457 viewers. Of the initial total of 1,919 reviews posted at Amazon.com, the site provides a count in which 723 (37.6 per cent) offer the maximum five-star rating, 247 (12.8 per cent) give four stars, 149 (7.7 per cent) give three stars, 228 (11.8 per cent) offer two stars and 572 (28.8 per cent) offer the lowest-available one-star rating (some of these complain at not being allowed to rate the film as zero-star).[60] The top two categories account for 50.5 per cent and the bottom two total 41.6 per cent, a clear minority occupying the most middle-ground rating offered to viewers; the (mean) average rating reported by Amazon of three stars is highly unrepresentative of the general tenor of opinion. A similar divergence of opinion is found in 'user comments' posted on the Internet Movie Database.[61] Out of a total of 1,694 comments, 657 (38.8 per cent) are classified as 'loved it' (a rating of eight out of ten stars or higher) and 598 (35.3 per cent) as 'hated it' (a rating below eight stars). Of the latter, 211 (12.5 per cent) give the lowest rating of one star and a total of 426 (27.3 per cent) rate the film five stars or lower (the IMDb classification of 'hated it' for anything up to 7.9 stars might seem somewhat skewed upwards, and this is the case for some respondents, but there remain many distinctly unimpressed reviews among those that award as high as six or seven stars). Among the positive responses, 360 (21 per cent) give the highest ten-star rating and 238 award nine stars, a total of 598 (35.3 per cent) placing the film in the top brackets. A general tendency in these responses appears to be for negative ratings to be more widely spread between the lower categories while the more positive tend to crowd into the two or three highest, as is reflected in the manner in which these are qualitatively classified by the IMDb. A more detailed breakdown of aspects of the Amazon responses is offered in the chapters that follow.

A general sense of the qualities – or 'quality' – of the film is evoked in these various fora through which *Lost in Translation* was mediated to the prospective viewer, from marketing materials to review coverage and viewer responses. An impression of broad audio-visual texture is given in the trailer, although much less so in the main poster/cover artwork, and is also sketched verbally in most of the published reviews. The following chapters of this book examine these in more detail, in their own right but with an emphasis on the manner in which they contribute to the particular positioning of the film text in the industrial and cultural landscape. This process begins with analysis of some of the key frameworks through which the film might be expected to be understood and/or placed by viewers or against which it might be defined. The starting point, following on from the emphasis of the marketing strategy examined above, is the role of stardom, particularly in the case of Bill Murray, his performance and what exactly his presence contributes to the shape and status of *Lost in Translation*. This is followed by a consideration of the role of Coppola, as 'auteur' writer-director, and of the film's relationship to dominant genre frameworks, particularly its somewhat ambiguous positioning in relation to the romantic comedy format.

2. Frameworks: Stardom, Authorship, Genre

Stardom, Bill Murray: Mixing comic performance and sincerity

If *Lost in Translation* was originally written with Bill Murray in mind, and Murray figured most centrally in marketing devices such as the trailer and the main poster, the presence of the star is as good a place as any to begin the closer analysis of the film itself, and some of the key frameworks in which it might be expected to be located for viewers. Murray was an important ingredient in the production from a commercial point of view, as reflected by his prominence in the marketing campaign, which implies that his presence was considered to be one of the strongest selling points of the film. As an established star, with a track record over a period of more than two decades, he brought to *Lost in Translation* a number of associations on which the film plays, sometimes quite explicitly. These have a prominent role in some central narrative dimensions of the production, including the fact that Murray's character is a disillusioned performer engaged in what he is all too aware is a cynical cashing-in on his image (in contrast to what is signified by the actor's presence in the film). They also contribute importantly to the broader positioning of the film in the indie/Indiewood arena. The general location, and more specific performance, of Murray in *Lost in Translation* can be understood in itself as a manifestation of the kind of hybrid status that typically characterises the Indiewood sector. The film draws on two major trends in the career of the star: an earlier association with broad Hollywood comedy and a later move towards what were widely viewed as more 'serious' and substantial performances in the independent or Indiewood realms. These rather different sets of associations constitute a significant part of the intertextual web within which the film is situated, the aim of this chapter being to conduct a kind of triangulation of the position of *Lost in Translation* through its situation in relation to such frameworks.

Murray's early background and establishment as a star took place clearly in the dimension of comedy, of a generally broad variety. Starting in Chicago in the improvisational comedy troupe Second City, he gained wider attention in *The National Lampoon Radio Hour* from 1973 to 1974 before becoming a regular on the acclaimed *Saturday Night Live* television series in 1977. Two years later, his film career began with *Meatballs* (1979), the first of a number of comedies including *Caddyshack* (1980), *Stripes* (1981) and *Ghostbusters* (1984) that built upon his earlier work to establish a particular kind of screen comic persona, the latter a major box-office hit that raised Murray to the status of highly bankable star. The persona generated by Murray through these and other films is usually characterised in terms of the deployment of a distinctive attitude and set of mannerisms: a wry, sardonic delivery often accompanied by deadpan looks at other characters.

The extent to which Murray's film performances have been rooted in a particular comic persona of this kind is of direct relevance to broader frameworks within which stardom has been examined, both generally and in more specific relation to comedy, and how these might apply in the case of *Lost in Translation*. A binary opposition is suggested by Barry King, in a much-cited essay, between what he terms 'impersonation' and 'personification'.[1] 'Impersonation' implies what might generally be considered to be 'proper acting', which is to say a kind of performance in which the actor seeks to transcend his or her own personality, to 'disappear' into the character-role. 'Personification', in contrast, suggests the development of a particular persona associated with the performer from one role to another; the cultivation of an identifiable group of personal-performative traits and their deployment across a career. The former, bearing associations with more 'serious' drama, is generally accorded higher cultural and critical status. 'Personification' is conventionally viewed as inferior, according to dominant cultural hierarchies, suggesting lack of 'real' acting ability or what is implied to be a 'cheaper' or 'lazier' form of performance in which the star relies primarily on the manifestation of his or her own characteristics rather than performing the kind of work required for impersonation/transformation (even if the persona itself should be understood as a construct, a performed version of the 'self', rather than a naked display of individual personality).

The distinction between impersonation and personification (not always as clear-cut as the above sketch might imply) has a particular currency in the arena of film comedy, where a parallel tension can be identified between what are understood as 'performative' and 'narratively-integrated' realms. From their beginnings in the early twentieth century to date, comedy formats have manifested rival pulls between comic performances – as attractions in their own right – and the situation of such performances within narrative frameworks.[2] In some types of comedy, the emphasis is on a fragmented series of comic performances only weakly if at all integrated into an overarching narrative sequence (a tendency found in examples ranging from early slapstick to many recent or contemporary movie spoofs); in others, comedy emerges largely from narrative situation (as in many examples of satire or romantic comedy). The 'comedian comedy' has been identified as a feature format in which the persona of a particular comic performer (or in some cases, group of performers) is more or less integrated into a narrative of the 'classical Hollywood' variety, a largely coherent narrative constructed on the lines of successive cause/effect sequences that make broadly logical sense.[3] In some cases, comedian comedies demonstrate hybrid qualities, evenly balancing the dimensions of comic-personal performance and its narrative situation.

Bill Murray's career can be situated in relation to these frameworks in a manner that typifies a not-uncommon dynamic. It manifests a shift, over time, from emphasis on the comic and/or performative/personification towards impersonation and greater narrative integration (the latter two are often viewed as connected, sustained character-centred performance tending to be narrative-oriented). This involves, in the process, a general movement 'up' the cultural hierarchy, as underlined by the accompanying shift from the mainstream/Hollywood to the more 'select' indie or Indiewood sectors. This is a dynamic in which Murray's performance in *Lost in Translation* occupies a strategic position, in its balancing of different qualities, although the overall shift should be understood as part of a broader, less one-dimensional process.

How exactly, then, has the balance between these different dimensions of performance been manifested in Murray's career, up to, playing into and beyond *Lost in Translation*? Early films such as *Meatballs*, *Stripes* and *Ghostbusters* provide plenty of opportunities for characters played by Murray to engage in performative antics. The tendency is towards an anarchic, disruptive presence, as is the case with a great many comedian comics in film, from the Marx Brothers to Mr Bean. In *Meatballs*, Murray plays a summer-camp counsellor set up against an ineffectual authority figure. In *Stripes* he is the slob new recruit who antagonises the drill sergeant, playing into a long tradition of service comedies. In *Ghostbusters*, again, he brushes up against authority and leaves a trail of devastation in the wake of himself and his team. It is worth noting, though, that in each of these cases the Murray character is also positioned as a mediating figure between anarchy and order, performing a leadership role among the lower and more disruptive orders. Much of his presence in *Meatballs* consists of brief performative pieces, particularly a range of put-on voices, mock attitudes and affected speeches, in which he is cast in the role of a kind of informal performer-within-the-fiction. This is material broadly reminiscent of his performances in *Saturday Night Live*, albeit here motivated by a more consistently located character/ plot framework. Similarly performative verbal routines are mobilised in *Stripes* and *Ghostbusters*, although to a reduced extent in each case. It is in these two performances in particular, increasingly in *Ghostbusters*, that the sardonic/deadpan dimension of his existing persona is reinforced.

A film often identified as an initial turning point in Murray's career, towards a more dramatically grounded dimension amid its comic or performative elements, *en route* to his later indie or Indiewood roles, is *Groundhog Day* (1993). This is something of an over-simplification, given that he had made earlier forays more deeply into the realm of impersonation, namely *Where the Buffalo Roam* (1980) and *Razor's Edge* (1984). In the former he plays 'gonzo' journalist Hunter S. Thompson, giving a highly mannered performance, loud and disruptive, but significantly more 'in character' than his other work of the time. The latter, a Somerset Maugham adaptation, offers a blend of 'Bill Murray'-style clowning and avowedly more 'serious' dramatic performance that was deemed, by general critical consensus, not to have worked (according to the established version, the role was Murray's price to the studio, Columbia Pictures, for his agreement to appear in *Ghostbusters*). Neither was considered a success, either critically or commercially, which might account for their less prominent role in perceptions of the performer's career trajectory. *Groundhog Day*, on the contrary, was a hit at both levels, and is widely seen as one of the high points of Murray's art. The scenario, in which Murray plays cynical weatherman Phil Connors, forced to live the same day over and over again, is another that affords plenty of scope for characteristic performative routines, especially given the opportunity to ring the changes, repeatedly, on the same actions and situations. A greater than usual degree of performance-related reflexivity is implied in the process. In previous roles, Murray characters had often performed within the diegesis – whether in mannered chat-up routines or attempts to taunt authority – but in this case a key dimension of the narrative is the chance Connors is given to try out different approaches towards his goals, chiefly the winning of the affections of producer Rita (Andie MacDowell).

Groundhog Day also provides more scope than most earlier Murray films for the development of emotional qualities presented as more serious or sincere. These are not entirely absent in the likes of *Meatballs, Stripes* and *Ghostbusters* (the former, providing perhaps Murray's most openly performative role, also includes a 'sincere' dimension in which his character befriends and supports the stereotypically shy boy at camp who is picked on by his contemporaries), but developed significantly further in this case. *Groundhog Day* has a stronger and far from implicit 'moral' stance as well, promoting the importance of overcoming selfishness in order to become a 'better' person and, unsurprisingly, to achieve life-goals as a result; see also *Scrooged* (1988), which combines a similar element of climactic moral transformation with highly demonstrative engagement of the Murray comic persona. The Murray performance of *Groundhog Day* is one that includes star-persona characteristics such as arrogance, egotism and demonstrative routines, but combined here with resonances constructed to suggest the 'caring' and the 'heart-felt', the structure of the film providing ample opportunity for the exercise of each. Comedy can be understood as a form – or, more properly, a modality – that offers a balance between comic distance from the world on screen (distance that permits us to sit back and enjoy the travails of the central characters) and a sense of greater implication in the diegetic universe (a vicarious emotional participation and allegiance with character).[4] Most comedies offer a combination of the two but the balance varies along a continuum from the most distanced slapstick to work that blurs the line between comedy and the more avowedly dramatic, serious or tragic. Some degree of implication is offered in examples such as Murray's broadest early comedies, but the balance is shifted significantly further in this direction in *Groundhog Day*, and to an increased extent in some of the work that followed.

The most significant milestone in Murray's career up to *Lost in Translation*, by what appears to be a critical consensus, is *Rushmore* (1998), the film that launched a process through which the performer became associated with works of a distinctly indie or Indiewood character.[5] On industrial grounds, *Rushmore* is a studio picture, produced and distributed by divisions of the Disney empire (Touchstone Pictures and Buena Vista Pictures, respectively) on a $20 million budget. In tone and attitude, however, it has an indie feel – the tale of an awkward, quirky, underachieving prep school pupil, including his relationship with the rich industrialist played by Murray – and is very much the work of a distinctive imagination, that of writer-director Wes Anderson, for whom Murray was to become a regular player. *Rushmore* is the type of comedy that might be expected of the indie sector: that is to say, one in which the implication quotient is relatively high and the modality shifts between dry, understated humour and emotional discomfort. As far as Murray is concerned, the film has been taken generally to mark a clear – and successful – move into more 'mature' dramatic territory, not just in the playing of an older, disillusioned character, but in the nature of the performance itself. With the exception of a very brief performative moment, when his character is attacked by a swarm of bees in a hotel room, Murray gives a 'straight' dramatic performance: no quirks, no wry deadpan glances, little of what had become a familiar comic persona.

Rushmore was followed up by two smaller roles that have also been noted as part of the narrative of shifting career trajectory: that of a reactionary ventriloquist in Tim Robbins' Depression-era drama *Cradle Will Rock* (1999) and Polonius in Michael Almereyda's corporate-era updating of *Hamlet* (2000) – each designed as a 'serious' dramatic performance (a performer, but not 'performative', in the former; quite mannered but not in a typically 'Bill Murray' style in the latter). The next instalment in this process was Murray's appearance in a substantial secondary role in Anderson's *The Royal Tenenbaums* (2001, another Touchstone production), although it is important to note that this is a preferred reading that somewhat over-simplifies the picture. Between *Hamlet* and *Tenenbaums*, he also put in a performance that included a good deal of more traditionally Murray-style fooling-around comedy as Bosley in *Charlie's Angels* (2000), along with appearances in *Speaking of Sex* (2001) and *Osmosis Jones* (2001), the latter involving an extension of the 'slob' characteristics associated with early films such as *Stripes*. *The Royal Tenenbaums* seemed clearly to consolidate the position established by *Rushmore*, however, along with *Cradle Will Rock* and *Hamlet*. Murray again plays – straight – a middle-aged character whose life goes downhill. What started out in the late 1970s and into the 1980s as the deadpan, with a tendency towards the smirk, has shifted here towards the hangdog, the under-played evocation of sad loneliness. This appears to have gained the status effectively of a new Murray persona, deployed as a central component of *Lost in Translation* and again in leading roles in subsequent features such as Anderson's *The Life Aquatic with Steve Zissou* (2004) and arch-independent Jim Jarmusch's *Broken Flowers*.

At the time of *Lost in Translation*, then, Murray brought with him to the project a range of associations, but primarily falling into the two camps defined by his earlier comic persona and his more recent ventures into dramatic performance closer to the indie end of the cinematic spectrum. One of the striking features of the film is the extent to which it mobilises both of the dominant Murray-related frames of reference. It includes a number of performative or otherwise broadly comic routines – including some of those drawn upon so heavily in the trailer examined in the previous chapter – in addition to trading on and playing its own part in the development of Murray's reputation as a more serious performer, particularly in the subtle evocation of middle-aged life crisis. The film opens with Murray in underplaying, passive mode, narratively motivated through its location in his jet-lagged arrival in Tokyo. Some drolly delivered lines follow, when he is met and greeted by an excessively large number of overly attentive hotel personnel, a blank expression of the kind particularly characteristic of this phase of his career (developed further in *Broken Flowers*) being deployed in scenes in which he towers over fellow occupants of a lift and is subsequently found sitting silently on his bed. An obvious instance of comic business, although played low-key, is inserted in a sequence the following morning in which he attempts to use a shower that appears incapable of adjustment to meet his height (a second not-very-subtle joke about the diminutive stature of the Japanese).

The first of two overtly performative sequences follows shortly afterwards, some nine minutes into the film, when Murray's character shoots his commercial for Suntory whisky. A good deal of comic mileage is extracted from the process of translation – lengthy exchanges in Japanese being reduced to very brief phrases of English – to which the star's principal contribution is a series of puzzled/concerned expressions, establishing a state of bemusement that typifies Bob's response to much of the local texture he experiences during the film. A distinctly performative mode is entered when Murray delivers his lines to camera, in a somewhat smug, affected manner, although only briefly and subject to the frantic 'cutto, cutto, cutto' of the over-excited director. Back in his hotel room, further bemused expressions follow, in response to the apparent oddities of Japanese television (including a dubbed sequence involving a much younger Bill Murray that appears to have been taken from *Saturday Night Live*). A seemingly unmotivated sequence of broader comedy comes after seventeen minutes, with the visit of the 'lip my stockings' woman, during which Murray's performance moves from further bemused puzzlement to physical antics, as the character is twice pulled to the floor by the crazy behaviour of his visitor, eventually breaking a light-fitting (at which point the action cuts away, to Bob eating later in the hotel restaurant).

The most sustained performative sequence follows a few minutes later, during a still-photography shoot. Murray/Bob engages in a number of sardonic wisecracks during and in between the striking of a sequence of poses/attitudes, as requested by the photographer. He is asked to do a 'mysterious face', to put his hand 'close his face' and to do impressions of the 'lat pack' and 'Loger Moore', to which Murray, in tuxedo and a touch of mascara, responds with a series of mannered smiles, off-centred grins, angled tilts of the head and other stylised expressions. In the wise-cracks, general attitude and the striking of poses, this seems closer to the stuff of earlier Murray routines, although it is given clear narrative motivation through the fact that Bob is a professional performer and is 'on stage' for the sequence in the diegesis. It is worth noting how the more performative sequences in the film – the two on-set shoots – are presented visually to the viewer. It is not uncommon, in the performative tradition, for comic routines to be presented more or less directly to the viewer, either through direct address – in which the presence of the viewer is acknowledged – or more commonly through framing routines in which material is presented directly (or very close to directly) without any explicit acknowledgement of the process.

Murray's performance for the commercial is presented directly to the viewer of *Lost in Translation* (as well as to its fictional audience), although in a reflexive manner that draws attention to its existence *as* a filmed/constructed act. Murray/Bob delivers a single line, twice, with much untranslated instruction from the director in between. On each occasion it is given directly to the viewer, the impression at that moment being that diegetic and extra-diegetic cameras are the same; that is to say, we see exactly what the viewer of the completed commercial would see. This is surrounded, however, by more distant shots and other perspectives in which the two camera views are clearly separated, as would be expected in a 'back-stage' sequence of this kind. Immediately before Murray's first delivery of his line within the fiction, a camera situated further back from the stage on which he sits pans to show a video monitor – capturing the

Figure 4 Performative mode: Murray/Bob delivers his commercial line directly to diegetic and non-diegetic cameras. © 2003 Universal Studios

Figure 5 The performance mediated within the fictional frame. © 2003 Universal Studios

view of the diegetic camera – which fills one side of the screen. No such device is used in the case of the second delivery. The key moments in which Murray's performance is crystallised are presented immediately and performatively to the viewer of *Lost in Translation*, offering the brief pleasure of the performance in itself, but in each case this is closely framed by explicit and more extended acknowledgment of its status as a construct.

A similarly hybrid status can be identified in the framing of the longer still-photography shoot. Murray sits on a stool, directly facing the movie camera, but directing his performance slightly off to the viewer's right, towards the direction of the fictional photographer. The position of the latter is established in longer and mid-shots from behind his back. Most of the performance is given in the closer, frontal shot, but the bulk of the 'Roger Moore' routine is shot from the mid-shot position behind the photographer, with his silhouette appearing in the foreground. The effect is, again, a qualified or partial form of direct performance, a feature typical of many comedian comedies in which a balance is achieved between the maintenance of a degree of 'playing out' towards or close to the position of the viewer and location within the confines of a self-sufficient fictional universe.[6] An additional dimension is contributed to the impression of distance from the performance by the diegetically established attitude of the Murray character in these sequences: painfully aware that he is selling-out by accepting a huge sum of money for doing such endorsements when he might be putting his talents to more worthwhile ends ('I could be doing a play somewhere'). This adds to the manner in which the film itself hedges around the delivery of the performative routines to us. It increases the sense of distanciation, from one perspective, but the viewer is still directly being sold the Bill Murray persona doing his thing. This is another level on which the film can be understood to be 'having it both ways', in what might be a typically Indiewood manner: it offers to the viewer the more immediate pleasure of the performative acts, but situated in a manner that enables these also to be deconstructed to some extent.

There are other sequences in *Lost in Translation*, beyond these diegetic performances, in which Murray offers material closer to the performative end of scale. In one of the relatively early exchanges between Bob and Charlotte in the hotel's 'New York' bar, what is marked as a more 'ordinary' conversation slips into one speech that functions as a kind of mini-routine, albeit in a low-key manner, as Bob jokingly undercuts the longevity of his 25-year marriage:

You sleep one-third of your life. That knocks off eight years of marriage right there, so you're down to 16 and change – you know, you're just a teenager at marriage; you can drive it, but there's still the occasional accident.

This is framed, again, in a manner that seems to sit somewhere between direct delivery and total integration into the fictional world, although closer to the latter. Most of the speech is given in a two-shot of Bob and Charlotte. She is in the left foreground, the back of her head to the camera and out of focus (there is also a shift to a reverse-angle view of her, however). He sits with his body at a 45-degree angle to the camera (mid-way between facing the screen and facing out of shot to the right). His head is turned to the left most of the time to face closer towards the position of the camera while his eyes turn further left to meet those of Charlotte (both head and eyes position shift somewhat during the sequence). The routine is played out towards the viewer to some extent, as before, but in a manner that falls well short of being a direct performative address. It is notable that much the same framing and staging is used shortly beforehand and afterwards in parts of the scene in which the discourse seems more ordinary/everyday, rather than a clear shift being made in the relatively more performative moments. This kind of decoupage is also frequently used more generally in cinema to establish a point of address that seems to lie somewhere between the positions occupied by diegetic and extra-diegetic viewers or auditors; it is not, in itself, sufficient to mark out clearly the performative dimension of the routine.

What might be seen as the most arbitrary inclusion of broad comic material is the sequence in which Bob struggles with an out-of-control exercise machine, a standard physical-comedy routine for which little specific motivation is provided (although it does fit into the wider 'problems of translation' framework, the character being unable to understand the Japanese-language instructions barked electronically by the machine). This is not a particularly Murray-associated routine, falling into a broader category of 'human-against-machine' that has been a staple of film comedy at least as far back as Chaplin's *Modern Times* (1936), but its place in the film seems most explicable as a general intertextual nod to Murray's comic background. There is no question, in this case, of a performative framing towards the viewer, the sequence being seen from a position three-quarters behind/beside or alongside the action, although it does occur in the otherwise isolated space (another factor sometimes in performative staging) of an empty hotel gym.

Otherwise, *Lost in Translation* contains plenty of moments in which Murray's lines, actions and/or delivery seem to fit, broadly, into aspects of his established comic persona, particularly in a drollness of delivery and one or two other minor routines (some business surrounding Charlotte's bruised 'black/brack toe' in a sushi bar; a somewhat

eccentric exchange of mutually impenetrable comments and arm gestures with an elderly man at the hospital visited for treatment). There is,
however, a distinct shift of tone, overall, in the latter half of the film. The
balance of Murray's performance moves towards the more 'serious' and
'sincere' ends of the spectrum, as Bob and Charlotte become increasingly drawn to one another and as the film attends more explicitly to
the issues of loneliness and uncertainty with which it engages. It is striking, for example, that when Bob takes part in a karaoke session, after
'escaping' the hotel with Charlotte and a group of her friends from the
city (approximately mid-way through the film), this diegetically performative moment is not treated as such by the film itself. The camera
on Murray remains at something like a 90-degree angle, sidelong to a
performance that is directed unambiguously into the fictional space. The
camera also wanders, during these numbers, away from Murray and to
other characters in the scene, including a shift of focus to concentrate
on Charlotte in the background and a 'meaningful' exchange of looks
between the two. This is marked, within the fiction, as a distinctly 'off-
camera' experience, something heart-felt and far more authentic than
the whisky endorsements or some of Bob's other more throw-away lines
or attitudes.

The same can be said of a number of other sequences involving
the two principals in the second half of the film. Murray plays entirely
straight in a key bonding scene in which the pair hole up in Charlotte's
hotel room one night during the period when her husband is out of the
city on a photo-shoot. They drink sake, watch *La Dolce Vita* (1960) on
television and talk more deeply about substantial personal issues: her
uncertainty about what to do with her life, to which he offers advice; his
relationship with his wife and children. There are no 'lapses' into comic
or mannered routines in any of this, no markers of greater-than-usual
distance. This is presented as the stuff of serious dramatic engagement,
in which the viewer is offered the prospect of substantial emotional
implication, and it becomes the dominant tone of the latter parts of *Lost
in Translation*, through to a period in which the pair have a falling-out
(after he sleeps with the hotel lounge-singer) before re-establishing their
connection and finally parting (elements to be considered in more detail
below in relationship to genre frameworks).

In enacting such a shift in the dominant tenor of Murray's performance, the film itself seems to mirror his broader career trajectory. The
turn towards an emphasis on what is presented as 'sincere' engagement

Figure 6 'Sincerity' of performance: Bob sings into the fictional space, watched by Charlotte. © 2003 Universal Studios

Figure 7 'Heartfelt' 1: Bob's look towards Charlotte. © 2003 Universal Studios

Figure 8 'Heartfelt' 2: her return. © 2003 Universal Studios

seems particularly telling in the case of Murray, a performer whose earlier persona was at least partly based on a notion of the opposite: the 'patent insincerity' cited by Pauline Kael in a review of *Ghostbusters*, or the 'trademark insincerity' identified by another critic in relation to his career up to and including *Groundhog Day*.[7] The fact that the karaoke singing sequence is situated so clearly as within the 'sincere' register seems particularly significant given that the performances that marked Murray's breakthrough in *Saturday Night Life*, after what was generally considered to be a slow start when he joined the series, were his mocking turns as a figure who sings and introduces guests while taking a shower and his regular routine as the smoothly insincere 'Nick the lounge singer'.

Beyond the mix of associations from his earlier films, Murray also brought to *Lost in Translation* his talents in improvisation, an aspect of his work developed from the early-career stage of his time with Second City in Chicago. Improvised contributions were made to key sequences in both the more explicitly performative and 'sincere' dimensions of his characterization of Bob Harris, including the photography-shoot impressions and the karaoke session. Murray is also credited by Coppola with suggesting the sequence on the exercise machine during the later stages of the writing of the script. Apart from his general prominence in reviews, Murray's presence was one of the factors that marked the film to many critics as an early contender for the awards season, a status based primarily on the more subtle/serious/dramatic resonances of his performance and the sense of distance and development this implied from his comic persona.[8]

Bill Murray's presence in *Lost in Translation* figures substantially in the Amazon viewer responses, as might be expected from his general star-currency as well as his prominence in the film and its marketing and critical reception. Murray is cited by 823 out of 1,900 postings, or 43 per cent of the sample. This falls to 38 per cent if we remove the 94 instances in which his name is used as a substitute for that of the character, a quite frequent occurrence in such responses, rather than in specific reference to the performer as such. Of those who make a judgement about his performance, favourable responses are in the clear majority, totalling 571. This is 30 per cent of the total sample, 78 per cent of the Murray citations that are not just references to the character, or 86.6 per cent of those which express a clear opinion about the nature of his performance (88 reviewers make a negative judgement while 198 offer neutral or balanced responses or ones in which no specific judgement is offered about Murray's role in the film). The positive responses take a number of forms, ranging from very brief adjectival phrases ('brilliant', 'wonderful', etc.) to more considered or substantial comments about the specific nature of the performance or its place in Murray's broader career trajectory. A number of the latter situate it positively in the kind of narrative outlined above and by many professional critics. As one puts it: 'This reinvention of Murray (which started in Rushmore, was polished in The Royal Tenenbaums and will be furthered in The Life Aquatic. Thank you Wes Anderson) is a marvel to watch and through Lost in Translation is worthy of the Best Actor Oscar' (Edwin B. Arnaudin, Brevard, NC, United States, 7 January 2004).[9] Another refers to the film as a 'triumphant comeback' for Murray: 'Though well known as a comedian, he shines in this dramatic role' (David Anderson, St Cloud, MN, 8 February 2004). Others put their praise in terms of qualities more widely associated with the star, for example: 'Bill Murray is superb with his trademark bemused expressions' (Nial Westwood, London, UK, 25 February 2004).

Murray gets the prominence of first mention, either in the body of the text or the heading, in 94 responses (4 per cent of the total or 12 per cent of those who cite the performer other than just in reference to the character he plays), although the tone of these is highly varied. Some put their praise up front, and make it either the main focus of the response or one of these. But a substantial number express disappointment, on a range of counts. In some cases, the name of the star, and the associations it carries, set up the wrong expectations: of more straightforward comedy or a more familiar 'Bill Murray' performance. Many offer praise for the performer but in the context of negative criticism of the film itself, representative examples including one that offers the heading 'Bill Murray . . . yes . . . rest . . . no' ('joostusa', Charleston, Ill, 14 April 2004) and another that begins: 'I am a huge fan of Bill, and think he is funny in everything he does, but even he couldn't help me get through one of the most boring movies EVER' (Benjamin Corona, Dallas, Texas United States, 2 April 2004) (for more on many responses that declare the film to be 'boring', see the narrative section in the following chapter). Entirely negative judgements of Murray's performance are fewer in number. Some suggest that he does not really 'act' in the film, but merely plays himself, although for others the fact that he does not *appear* to be acting is taken as a positive. Much of the evaluative discussion is related to the awards nominations and/or general critical praise received by the star, one of the most negative conclusions being: 'The performances everyone talks about . . . simply aren't there. Bill Murray's worse performance EVER . . . he doesn't laugh, doesn't cry, doesn't even alter his facial expression the ENTIRE MOVIE!' ('blackmosesi2', Salt Lake City, Utah, 6 March 2004).

Before leaving the subject of stardom, it is also necessary to say something about the role of Scarlett Johansson, whose performance is clearly a very central component of *Lost in Translation* and also gets appreciation from substantial numbers of critics and Amazon respondents. I am giving much less prominence to Johansson in this section because her presence – however effective – is likely to have played a smaller part in the shaping of frameworks-of-expectation around the film, both in advance and during viewing, even if the film marked a major breakthrough in the development of her career. The primary associations brought by Johansson were from the indie world, although in parts that were much less likely to have added up to a familiar persona/presence for more than a minority audience. The films for which she was known at the time were the low-budget *Manny and Lo* (1996), the mainstream Robert Redford studio production *The Horse Whisperer* (1998) and the relatively high-profile indies, *The Man Who Wasn't There* and *Ghost World* (both 2001). Her performance in *Lost in Translation* brought a greater degree of prominence, reinforced by the release later in the same year of *The Girl with a Pearl Earring*. The dominant association across these roles (with the exception of *Ghost World*) is that of a girl or teenager of greater maturity than suggested by her years.[10] In *Manny and Lo* she is the more sensible although the younger of two sisters 'on the run' after escaping from foster parents. In *The Horse Whisperer* she is a teenager injured in a riding accident, playing moody and disaffected, as she does in *Ghost World* as the more negative and sneering of a pair of 'cynical' teens. The Johansson persona in *Lost in Translation* has recognisable components from each of the latter: it includes some of the moodiness evoked by both performances, although with more dimensionality (more light and shade) than her role in *Ghost World* and a range of brooding poses and looks in *The Horse Whisperer* similar to those deployed in Coppola's film. In *The Man Who Wasn't There*, Johansson, as a teenage pianist sought by the central character as a belated source of unfulfilled redemption, is a glowing symbol of purity and innocence amid the twists of low-key film noir. Overall, *Lost in Translation* seems to play a good deal on previously established Johansson role/persona traits – fresh-faced innocence/purity, vulnerability, youth-but-with-mature-depths – even if the resonances of these from earlier performances might be available to only a relative minority of viewers. As Charlotte, Johansson offers plenty of the innocent and vulnerable, with her usual pale complexion and doe-eyed looks. She is sometimes sleepy/jet-lagged, often wearing puzzled expressions during her wanderings around Tokyo. In the first such sequence, her dark coat worn over a short skirt, untucked shirt and jumper give her the look of a schoolgirl. Hanging around in her hotel room, often alone, she tends towards tops and underpants that give her a vulnerable appearance, especially so when sitting exposed in the large picture window. There are distinct resonances of the 'little girl lost and confused', although this is played in conjunction with sequences in which she is presented as more mature, confident and knowing. The latter qualities are most to the fore in her engagements with Bob and the comparison the film draws between Charlotte and Kelly (Anna Faris), a 'ditzy' Hollywood actress, issues to which we return below in the context of generic frameworks.

Auteurism, Sofia Coppola: A distinctive presence?

While Bill Murray had a long career and a persona established well in advance of his appearance in *Lost in Translation*, the writer-director came to the film with only a single feature under her belt, which might be expected to reduce the extent to which it was likely to be understood via the filmmaker as 'auteur' or distinctive authorial presence. Sofia Coppola's career as a filmmaker at the time was restricted to a few shorts and music videos, a co-authorship credit for the screenplay of her father's contribution to the three-part *New York Stories* (1989) and her feature debut, *The Virgin Suicides*. Coppola had strong 'name' recognition, however, given the potency of the family identity, even if that might at times have appeared a handicap (with potential implications of nepotism). The name-recognition factor was sufficient to gain more than usual journalistic attention to her work, although *The Virgin Suicides* was received positively enough to have sparked some interest in her next feature without the dynastic connection. If Coppola was pushed to the margins in promotional forms such as the main poster and trailer, almost entirely in favour of Murray's presence, the same could not be said of the work of many critics and feature writers, as indicated in the previous chapter. Coppola provided another substantial hook onto which film-related journalists could hang the film, and thus a framework potentially

Figure 9 Auteur at work? Sofia Coppola directs Bill Murray on the set of *Lost in Translation*. © 2003 Universal Studios

available to viewers. The film was, clearly, a work primarily of her individual creation, as writer and director, and rooted in aspects of her own personal experience. She certainly qualifies as auteur in that literal sense. The main question to be addressed in this section is the extent to which, beyond such facts of origination and production, *Lost in Translation* might be understood as a distinctly 'Sofia Coppola' film – bearing her distinctive marks – according to the more specific manner in which the term 'auteur' has been used in film studies, and how far such an understanding might be available to viewers.

The granting of auteur status in the critical/analytical sense usually requires the identification of distinctive traits that mark out a body of work from the industrial norm, the concept first having been defined in this manner in relation to the products of a select group of filmmakers from the studio era. Auteur status of this kind implies a more 'artistic' approach, to some extent, even if manifested from within an industrialised system. For Andrew Sarris, a key figure in the popularisation of the approach in the United States, it implies a Romantic notion of the artist achieving a transcendence of the system from within, a quality

defined in his view specifically by the level of constraint posed by the
studio production line.[11] The mark of the auteur is usually identified at
two levels: the pursuit of distinctive themes or issues, across a body of
work; and the presence of distinctive formal traits that act as what Sarris
terms the director's 'signature'.[12] Ideally, the two should combine, form
embodying content, although this is often far from so neatly the case.
Taken more generally, auteurism could be marked by departures from
the mainstream norm or by a consistent favouring of particular identifiable options within the norm.[13] As far as Sofia Coppola is concerned,
the principal test at the time of *Lost in Translation* would be a comparison
with *The Virgin Suicides*. From a slightly longer perspective, we might also
include her next feature, *Marie Antoinette* (2006), although this is clearly
not a factor that was in play at the original time of release; such temporal
factors might be complicated, however, by home viewing – numerically,
the dominant mode of consumption – in which films are far from always
watched in historical sequence. It is also possible to include Coppola's
early shorts and music videos, along with the screenplay for *New York
Stories*, although these seem less likely to have been available as points of
reference in the consumption and reception of *Lost in Translation* for other
than a small minority.

   In what respects, then, could *Lost in Translation* be identified as a
product from the same filmmaker as *The Virgin Suicides*? There are some
points of similarity, although perhaps rather broad in nature. Both
feature teenage girl characters (or early twenties in the case of Charlotte
in *Lost in Translation*, although played by Johansson at eighteen) who are
bathed in a kind of transcendent beauty and given what is constructed
as a captivating appeal. These qualities are most explicitly developed in
The Virgin Suicides, as part of the body of the narrative, but Johansson is
presented to some extent in a similarly glowing light in *Lost in Translation*.
Each involves a coming-of-age component, albeit rather different; the
Lisbon girls of *The Virgin Suicides* all end up dead, while Charlotte is a
good few years older (coming-of-age is also a somewhat widespread literary and cinematic fictional trope, and so not the strongest of grounds
for identifying distinctive thematics). A stronger source of continuity
between the two is the centrality to each of what might be defined as
'mood' or 'atmospherics', qualities considered more closely in relation
to *Lost in Translation* in the following chapter. Both are 'mood pieces',
to a larger extent than is usual in either mainstream or indie cinema.
Each relies centrally on the evocation of impressions of aching loss and/

or need for connection. *The Virgin Suicides* invests strongly in the creation of a sense that the Lisbon girls represent something unfathomable and unobtainable to the group of boys with whom they come briefly into contact and who seek to grasp the mystery of their self-inflicted deaths. Something of the fleeting aspect of these qualities is also found in *Lost in Translation* (the theme of loneliness and search for meaning and connection is considered in Chapter 4).

As far as their formal dimensions are concerned, both films rely particularly on music in the creation of their atmospherics, another issue considered in more detail in the following chapter. It is significant that the same figure was employed in each case as music supervisor and/or producer, Brian Reitzell, while the group Air, which provided much of the soundtrack for the first film, reappears in one track in the second. Repeated use of the same collaborators, in what remains a largely collaborative medium, is another more qualified mark of the auteur and one that has a particular currency in the case of Coppola, who has benefited from connections with a network of film-related and other creative individuals, including but not limited to associates of her father.[14] Specific aspects of visual style might differ between the two films, but these include in both cases what are presented as 'dreamy' somewhat narcotised sequences (including, in *The Virgin Suicides*, the hazy, golden images that characterise the dramatisation of passages from the diary of Cecilia, the first of the girls to commit suicide). Each might be defined, up to a point, as including certain 'poetic' or expressive qualities, sometimes taking the place of more conventional/mainstream narrative development, although these are narratively located rather than resembling any more radical kind of cinema-poetry (as might be found in some instances of the avant-garde, for example). These qualities are used, in part, to offer something like a fetishistic representation of teenage girlhood, as embodying a quietly transcendent kind of beauty.

For major US critics, mediating the film to the first tier of viewers, the presence of *The Virgin Suicides* as an explicit point of reference was variable: sometimes a major point of departure for reviews, sometimes not present at all. The two main trade papers typified this division: *Variety* makes a direct comparison in its first line ('Adopting the same dreamily lyrical approach that distinguished her 1999 debut "The Virgin Suicides", Sofia Coppola generates an even further out-of-body feeling with "Lost in Translation"') while *The Hollywood Reporter* ignores Coppola's previous work altogether.[15] *The New York Times* makes reference to the fact that *The Virgin Suicides* 'was informed more substantially by the score by the group Air than by the narrative', but makes no direct comparison with the centrality of 'mood' music to *Lost in Translation*.[16] The *Los Angeles Times* cites Coppola's debut in the third paragraph but also offers no comparison between the two.[17] Much the same goes for the *New York Post* in another positive review that refers to *The Virgin Suicides* only as 'beautifully shot but overpraised'.[18] *USA Today* goes as far as to suggest that 'This movie isn't anything like *Suicides*', contrary to the view expressed in some other major regional/city dailies.[19] The *San Francisco Chronicle* opens its review with a strong reference to *The Virgin Suicides* and gives plenty of credit to Coppola for the style of *Lost in Translation*, but is another example in which no direct comparison is offered. It may be, of course, that viewers could do some of the work themselves to relate comments about the former more directly to the latter. This is done explicitly by both the *Chicago Tribune* and the *Seattle Post-Intelligencer*. The former begins by stating that Coppola has already, in her brief career, 'established herself as a remarkably intuitive director.'[20] While most rely on structure, plot and dialogue as building blocks, 'Coppola seems to work through her material by feel. Both of her movies, her 2000 adaptation of Jeffrey Eugenides "The Virgin Suicides" and now "Lost in Translation", zero in on emotions and moods, making them uncannily vivid.' The latter suggests that Coppola's sophomore film 'is another exploration of delicate relationships and uncommunicated frustrations, this one in a beautifully composed atmosphere of isolation.'[21]

Readers of any of these reviews would be left with a clear sense that *Lost in Translation* was a distinctly 'Sofia Coppola' production in general terms, as suggested above, and in numerous specific articulations of a distinct quality given to the film. How much that might include a sense of commonly shared features with *The Virgin Suicides* could depend on a number of factors, however, including whether or not they had seen or otherwise knew about the earlier film and the extent to which it was cited or used as an explicit point of comparison by critics. That *The Virgin Suicides* was not used as a point of reference in the trailer, posters or the DVD cover or accompanying text suggests that it was not seen as one of the most important hooks for potential viewers from a commercial perspective.

The addition of *Marie Antoinette* to her corpus increases the extent to which elements of *Lost in Translation* might be ascribed to a distinctive 'Sofia Coppola' factor, reinforcing some of what might appear to be more tenuous connections identified across her first two features. The fact that some elements identified in *Lost in Translation* and *The Virgin Suicides* might also be found in or clarified by a third film gives significantly greater ground for understanding them as more than just coincidence, even if any use of *Marie Antoinette* to help signify 'Coppola' in its predecessors has to be done with the caveat that this would only become apparent in retrospect. When *Marie Antoinette* is factored in, however, a potentially more clear-cut thematic dimension comes into focus: that of 'beautiful' young women effectively imprisoned or isolated in one way or another: the Lisbon girls, cooped up in their house and impenetrable to outside witnesses; Charlotte marooned in her hotel or distanced from most of her experiences of Tokyo life; and Marie Antoinette, initially at least, isolated amid the luxury and alien formalities of the royal palace at Versailles. Coppola has herself encouraged such a reading, describing *Marie Antoinette* in one interview as 'a continuation of the other two films' and the final chapter of a trilogy, although it is worth pointing out that the filmmaker tends to have a vested interest in playing up such connections as a way of establishing a 'trademark' identity that can be of value to the development of her career; a similar point can be made about critics, who might have an interest in identifying connections with earlier films as a way of demonstrating their 'expert' status.[22] Her central female protagonists are young and privileged in a manner that might be related to the filmmaker's own background, generally as well as in the more immediately biographical references in *Lost in Translation*.

Each film also includes a sense of looking-on at that which seems to repel by its surface sheen: the hazy world of the Lisbon girls, as experienced by their male contemporaries, and the overwhelming textures of Tokyo-neon and Versailles-extravagance (although in the latter two cases the protagonists eventually find some means of accommodation, if only temporary). A scene in *Marie Antoinette* shortly after the arrival of the central character at Versailles creates an impression of quiet, contemplative puzzlement that seems distinctly reminiscent of some of Charlotte's experiences in *Lost in Translation*. A later sequence, in which the Austrian-princess-become-queen-of-France (Kirsten Dunst) adopts a 'more simple, natural' white dress and sits amid long grass, buttercups and glowing sunlight, has strong resonances with the dreamy diary-based images from *The Virgin Suicides* cited above (although it might be argued that this is a more widely familiar trope, used for the evocation of lost or temporary moments of purity, innocence or respite). The greater-than-usual importance of music to the texture of the piece is another factor that can be seen to connect *Marie Antoinette* with its two predecessors and it is notable that Coppola again collaborates with Reitzell as music supervisor/producer. Some quietly lush guitar and keyboard atmospherics on the soundtrack are reminiscent of those employed in *Lost in Translation* (for example, in early sequences when Marie travels from Austria to France, as compared with the accompaniment to some of the passages in which Tokyo is viewed through the windows of taxis), although this film also ranges more widely in its musical points of reference, expressively mixing more immediately obvious classical pieces with the likes of Siouxsie and the Banshees, The Cure and Adam and the Ants.

What about Coppola's earlier works in film and music video? Her first credit of substance is for the co-authorship of her father's segment, 'Life without Zoe', in *New York Stories*, which centres around the life of a precocious 12-year-old who lives in a smart Manhattan hotel, her parents often being away travelling in pursuit of their artistic careers. Some parallel with Sofia Coppola's childhood experiences is apparent, the hotel that features in the film (the Sherry-Netherland) having been one of the family residences during her upbringing. The focus on a strikingly characterised near-teenage girl might appear to have some resonance with Coppola's subsequent features but any further grounds of comparison are limited. The characterisation of Zoe is bright and very matter-of-fact in manner, displaying none of the dreamy or seductive qualities found in *The Virgin Suicides* or *Lost in Translation*. Zoe seems to live mostly without her parents in a luxury hotel, but no significant parallel can be drawn on that basis with the scenario of *Lost in Translation*, if only because Zoe's status is far from isolated; she has a butler and is clearly well known to the hotel staff. (A hotel-setting theme might be consolidated by Coppola's fourth feature, *Somewhere*, shot in the summer of 2009, which features an actor's life of excess at the Chateau Marmont in Hollywood.[23]) A work more widely recognised as a launch-pad for Coppola's career as a filmmaker is her short film, *Lick the Star* (1998), which gained some currency by being broadcast on the Independent Film Channel and has also been available to view online on YouTube.[24]

Lick the Star is another teenage-girl-centred work, in this case featuring a clique of high-school students who hatch a plan to kill potential boy-pupil victims with rat poison (the title words playing as 'kill the rats' backwards). This seems a good deal closer to Coppola's subsequent feature work in several respects. It opens – like early scenes in *Lost in Translation* and *Marie Antoinette* – with images of one of the girls looking out of a moving vehicle window, followed by her perspective of passing suburban houses. The short is generally quite stylish, sometimes employing low angles, and seems particularly to have something in common with the later features in its frequent reliance on music as a major source of orchestration of images or events (although this is far from uncommon in portrayals of teen culture). One of the girls also makes a suicide attempt, after being ostracised by her peers, which suggests an obvious point of contact with Coppola's first feature. As far as connections established via collaborators are concerned, the film marks Coppola's first work with cinematographer Lance Acord, who subsequently performed the same role, central to the visual style of any production, on *Lost in Translation* and *Marie Antoinette*. There are also considerable differences, however, as with 'Life without Zoe'. Very little if anything exists here of the fetishised or romanticised portrayal of teenage (or post-teen) girls identified above. There is an emphasis on the question of teenage isolation vs belonging, in the shifting nature of who is or is not a member of the 'in' social group, but this is the typical material of teen/high-school films more generally and might also be seen as relatively thin ground for establishing auteur-based connections.

If we move on to consider music videos directed by Coppola, it is again possible to seek out some points of continuity across her wider body of work, but to engage in such a process is perhaps to stretch towards the limits of credibility. Her video for 'Shine' by Walt Mink (1993) features the band performing in the sunshine beside a pool and trampoline on which children play. A long-haired teenage blonde girl is among those highlighted during the track, twice depicted lying down on the grassy floor, an image that seems in retrospect to resonate with *The Virgin Suicides*. The video for 'This Here Giraffe' by The Flaming Lips (1996) also gives an important place to the figure of a young woman with long blonde hair, although most of the video is focused on the band itself. To try to fit these into an auteur-based narrative of recurring or consistent features is questionable, however, and only really suggested here as a way to highlight the problems that can result from such a process. Apart from anything else, such images of blonde young women have too great a currency in the wider culture – either as signifiers of innocence or sexuality, or some combination of the two – to be attributed solely or primarily to the distinctive mark of any individual cultural producer.

Coppola's other music videos up to and around the time of *Lost in Translation* offer little else to go on for an auteurist account. Two are based on footage from the features: Air's 'Playground Love' (2000) uses sequences from *The Virgin Suicides*, with the addition only of superimposed blobs of animated chewing gum, while 'City Girl' (2003) by Kevin Shields uses some footage not included in the final cut along with sequences from *Lost in Translation*. It might be pushing well beyond plausibility to imply any connection between the performance of the model Kate Moss in the video from 'I Just Don't Know What to Do with Myself' by the White Stripes (2003) – in which Moss, clad only in underwear, writhes and pole-dances in starkly lit monochrome – and anything else in Coppola's oeuvre. A long-haired 'beautiful' female figure, performing, isolated in the frame: it would be possible to make an argument that started along such lines, not to mention the potential resonances of the song title for the character of Charlotte; but would it be anything more than an auteur-obsessed over-reading?

As some of the above examples have demonstrated, increasingly so, there are dangers in auteur-based readings of films or other related works, even when they are the products of the same individual creator. It is entirely legitimate to identify what appear to be reasonably substantial continuities in subject matter, themes or formal dimensions, and to ascribe these to the distinctive presence of the auteur – up to a point. Rival explanations of recurrent elements of form or content can also be suggested in many cases, however, and it is not always clear at what point the auteur-based reading of particular detail ceases to be 'reasonable' or the continuities 'substantial'. It is by no means the case that every work by an individual should be expected to express something distinctive to that person, especially in relatively commercial and/or popular generic or other industrialised contexts. It is also important to distinguish between two dimensions of the process of seeking to identify auteur-related factors. On the one hand, they are considered in the sense of what seems to be *available* to be detected, read or read-into or across a series of works, the kind of exercise in which I have engaged in the preceding paragraphs. We also need to consider separately the extent to which an auteur-related dimension is likely to be a factor for viewers other than those actively seeking out such connections for the purposes of academic or other forms of explicit analysis – a key issue in the context of this chapter.

Some of the auteur-based connections outlined above might be likely to be mobilised by some viewers on the basis of their viewings of the films alone and/or in the context of connections highlighted by some critical reviews (or in word-of-mouth or internet-communicated associations generated through media such as blogs and social networking sites). Others might be less likely to have much if any currency in this domain. Any resonances from music videos not directly related to the film, such as they are, seem unlikely to be factors in the consumption and understanding of *Lost in Translation*, partly because of the limited nature of any such connections and also because their shared authorship (insofar as the director of a music video can be termed the author of a work also shaped strongly by the music and/or its creators) is likely to be known only to a minority of viewers. In the case of *Lick the Star* a connection might be available to some viewers, if still a small minority, given the more clearly Coppola-authored nature of the work and the fact that the film had the relative prominence of screenings on the Independent Film Channel and has been available on YouTube. It was also cited in the review of *Lost in Translation* in *The New York Times*, one of the most influential press sources, if only in passing, as signifying Coppola's 'interest in emotional way stations'.[25]

Auteur-based accounts also need to be qualified in many cases in relation to original source materials. *The Virgin Suicides* owes a great deal in its overall tone and mood to the novel by Jeffrey Eugenides of which it is generally a faithful adaptation. *Marie Antoinette* is based on a biography by Antonia Fraser, from which it takes much of its detail, although the dimension contributed by the filmmaker is more obviously apparent both in selection (from a much longer source, almost all of the broader historical context of which is ignored) and in the imposition of a distinctive tone and texture, including the use of music cited above. *Lost in Translation* is significantly different in being an original work by Coppola, although the classic case for auteurism argued by Sarris did more than just allow for the possibility of distinctive expression in the case of adapted work: the point for Sarris was that, under the studio system, the director's mark was more likely to be imposed at the level of form than content, because of the lack of control directors usually had in that context over their choice of projects on which to work. It is the *how* as much as or more than the *what* that is key to Sarris, and some who have followed his model, and there does appear to be some ground for identifying certain common characteristics in *The Virgin Suicides* and *Lost in Translation* (and, subsequently, *Marie Antoinette*) on this basis.

The pattern of viewer responses to the Coppola factor, as measured by

Amazon postings, is in some respects quite similar in shape to those on the subject of Bill Murray's presence in the film, although with a greater divergence of opinion. Coppola is cited by name by 609 respondents out of 1,900 (32 per cent). Another twenty-four cite her implicitly, via reference to the Coppola family or claims of nepotism, while six identify the filmmaker indirectly but not by name through reference to *The Virgin Suicides* and another one by reference to *Marie Antoinette* (taking the total to 640, or 33 per cent). A further ten make general reference of one kind or another to 'the director' without supplying any specific indication of her identity. These are lower proportions than those which identify Murray (about three-quarters of the Murray total), but by a smaller margin than might be expected, given the broader cultural currency usually possessed by stars in general and the fact that Murray's career was far more established at the time than that of Coppola. The relative prominence gained by Sofia Coppola can probably be attributed primarily to the currency of the family name, an issue addressed directly by a substantial minority of respondents, usually negatively, as will be seen below.

If Coppola's identity is one reference point for about one-third of the Amazon respondents, evaluative opinions are more divided than is the case for Murray. Positive evaluations are offered by 333 reviewers, 17.5 per cent of the total or 52 per cent of the 640 who directly or indirectly identify the filmmaker. As with comments about Murray, the nature of positive opinions varies between brief statements ('brilliantly directed', 'the talented Sofia Coppola', etc.) and more substantial articulations of the merits of her contribution. A relatively small number offer what I would interpret to be evidence of very strong investment in the filmmaker as a sustained and central point of positive focus, some twenty-five responses (1.3 per cent of the total or just under 4 per cent of those which identify her). Seventy reviews (3.6 per cent or 11 per cent) put Coppola at the start of the response or in the heading, although far from all of these are in the positive camp. Attempts to pin down what specifically makes for the 'Coppola' touch are quite limited, however, even in the responses that demonstrate the greatest investment in this dimension of the film. One of the strongest examples is the following:

Sofia Coppola's complex, beautiful, diverse sensibilities drench each frame with implications . . . revelations . . . perturbations . . . Like all perfect movies, this one is rich, deep, lavishly-textured, and gorgeously-layered. Coppola adds not a questionable jot nor extraneous tittle, and leaves out nothing necessary to her narrative or contemplation. She attends masterfully to imagery, editing, framing, character, dialogue, tension, narrative, symbol, improvisation, serendipity . . . a small sampling of her range of talents, may she live long and prosper in the movie-making business. (John Grabowski, USA, 9 September 2006)

No specific detail is given, typically, of what *exactly* constitutes the distinct sensibility: what exactly the nature is of the texture or layering or what exactly is 'masterful' about imagery, editing, framing or the like. Another, much shorter response, headed 'I love Sofia Coppola films', begins: 'I love to watch anything Sofia Coppola produces. She just has a unique view of love and friendship' (Thomas Nguyen, Corpus Christi, TX United States, 11 January 2007), but, again, nothing at all is said about the specific nature of this 'unique view'. One reviewer begins to point to a thematic strain in Coppola's work, but this too is an observation that remains undeveloped:

Considered in tandem with Coppola's previous film, The Virgin Suicides, we might in fact be seeing the emergence of a theme in her work concerning chaste relationships between members of the opposite sex who convey a profound sense of intimacy through small gestures. (Jason Kruppa, New Orleans, LA United States, 9 October 2003)

A sense that distinctive features can be identified in Coppola's two features of the time is also expressed in some less positive responses, as in the following, which begins:

'The Virgin Suicides' was a solid, though overrated directorial debut for Sofia Coppola. Moody, ethereal and meaningful, it presented a promising director and one to follow closely. With 'Lost in Translation', her sophomore effort, similarly gloomy and melancholic atmospheres persist, yet the movie doesn't quite work and fails to impress. (gonn1000, Portugal, 11 May 2004)

Such responses tend to make broad impressionistic statements, much like those found in the work of professional critics, as might be expected (it is clear from looking at Amazon responses to this and other films, and similar such postings on other sites such as the Internet Movie Database, that some viewers seek to write something with the appearance of a professional-style review, in contrast to others who offer responses marked more clearly as subjective, opinionated or fragmentary). One fact that emerges clearly from the Amazon sample is that *The Virgin Suicides* is the only other Coppola-related point of reference brought into play by respondents of this kind, cited by a total of 71 (3.7 per cent of the total or 11 per cent of those who identify the filmmaker). Only a single reference is made to *Marie Antoinette*, a response that says nothing of substance about the nature of the film or any qualities it might share with *Lost in Translation* ('. . . go see Mary [sic] Antoinette because it's hot and it ROCKS', Bodega Noriega, Brooklyn, 10 November 2006). No mention is made in any of the reviews of Coppola's short films or music videos, beyond a handful who comment on the 'City Girl' video provided as an extra on the DVD (one respondent demonstrates what seems to be a general unawareness of this dimension of Coppola's career by suggesting that, on the basis of the film, she 'would've been a great music video director' (Eugene, Columbus, OH United States), 2 February 2004).

Negative responses to Coppola's role in the production take a number of different forms that fall into two principal camps: general criticism in the context of her ability as a screenwriter or director (97 responses: 5 per cent of the sample or 15 per cent of those who identify the filmmaker) and criticism based to various degrees around notions of nepotism (72 responses: 3.7 per cent of the total or 11 per cent of those who identify Coppola by name or otherwise, including some who only identify her in terms of being a recipient of unfair advantage). The grounds for general criticism are varied, and not always clearly stated, one of the larger categories being negative opinion of the narrative substance or structure of the film, an issue considered in its own right in the following chapter. In some cases the criticism is sweeping, as in the following: 'A lot of praises of Sofia Coppola have been sung. Unfortunately, the film fails miserably in the departments she was responsible for' (MatterOfFact, United States, 24 June 2004). Accusations of nepotism vary from understated implication to outright claims, variously, that the film either would not have been funded/made, released, given such critical attention or received Academy Award nominations had it not been for the Hollywood family connections, a representative example stating that: 'Quite frankly, if Sofia Coppola, the writer and director of this film, were not the daughter of the legendary director Francis Ford Coppola, I am convinced that this film would have quickly vanished without trace. In fact, I doubt it would even have been made' (Lawyeraau, Balmoral Castle, 24 April 2004). A smaller number seek to rebuff such claims, one providing some details of the manner in which the film was funded (as discussed in Chapter 1), in response to suggestions that Coppola senior had also bankrolled the production.

Genre: *Not* a Romantic Comedy?

Lost in Translation contains elements of comedy, but it is not 'a comedy' in a sense that implies that comedy is a dominant modality, or that the category is sufficient to capture a full impression of the film. It also involves, centrally, a romance of a kind, but 'of a kind' has to be stressed. To ask, therefore, whether *Lost in Translation* can be understood as a romantic comedy, a pairing of the two categories, is to invite substantial qualification all round, although its relationship with the genre can usefully be understood as another key marker of its position in the cinematic spectrum. The film draws on some conventions familiar from romantic comedy, a format that dates back at least to the 1930s and flourished anew from the late 1980s through to the 2000s, but the manner in which it departs – including the non-consummation of the central relationship – is a prominent element of what distinguishes it from the mainstream. In this respect, *Lost in Translation* shares something with many indie or Indiewood features that use genre frameworks as points of partial departure: as familiar bases on which to build and as marker-points for degrees of variation from the norm.[26] The maintenance of a particular range of balance between the two is a characteristic feature of the indie and Indiewood landscapes. Initially most prominent in *Lost in Translation* appears to be the degree of departure, to the point at which it might be doubted whether the film really qualifies as a romantic comedy. This seems to be a conscious or close-to-conscious act of positioning, a denial that claims a particular (conventionally, 'higher') cultural standing: the status of that which lies, specifically, 'beyond' the simply generic. The film also depends for much of its narrative infrastructure, however, on more familiar generic devices, a consideration of which begins this section.

At the heart of *Lost in Translation* is the generation of an assumption that the central characters, Bob and Charlotte, have something fundamental in common: that they share something basic in what might loosely be characterised as their 'inner being'; that they are, ultimately, soul-mates of a kind, despite some obvious differences. The film is built around a process of bringing them together that has much in common with the defining armature of romantic comedy. There are substantial surface differences between the two, most obviously in age and experience, the potential overcoming of which is another romantic comedy staple. If the innate belongingness of the central couple is a cast-iron component of the genre, another is the existence of actual or potential 'wrong partner' figures for each, typically the fiancé/fiancée to whom one or both protagonists is erroneously committed, the diegesis revealing their ultimate incompatibility or unsuitability. This seems clearly the case with Charlotte and John in *Lost in Translation*, although less evidently with Bob and the off-screen presence of his wife Lydia (the voice of the film's costume designer, Nancy Steiner). The 'wrongness' of the fit between Charlotte and John has a thematic dimension of broader relevance to issues of cultural positioning, both within the diegesis and the extra-textual location of the film itself. John is allied to a world of what is presented as somewhat crass popular culture from which Charlotte remains distanced, through mechanisms discussed in greater detail towards the end of this section. No such clear distinction is suggested between Bob and Lydia, the strains in their relationship being attributed more to the accumulated effects of long-term marriage and the raising of children.

The sense of 'belonging together' that the film attributes to Bob and Charlotte is generated through a number of standard devices of a kind associated with romantic comedy. A core part of the structure of the film is constituted by a series of parallels and meetings between the two. A major component of this process is their shared experience of insomnia, the result of jet-lag. The particular quality of the experience is significant, contributing centrally to the manner in which the members of the couple are presented as sharing a separation and/or alienation from their surroundings. Insomnia functions as a specific shared experience, combined with the wider sense of puzzlement generated in relation to each character at the level of their engagement with seemingly 'strange' or alienating aspects of Japanese culture; the manner in which the protagonists are separated as a couple from their surrounding context is thus somewhat overdetermined. As insomniacs, Bob and Charlotte occupy a distinctive or special 'world apart', when most are asleep, variations of which are familiar currency in romantic comedy.[27] In this respect, their situations are paralleled early in the film, their sleeping difficulty exacerbated in each case by disturbances coming from their respective marriage partners. A sequence in which Bob lies awake and is then startled by the arrival of a fax from his wife is followed by one in which Charlotte's return to bed and attempt to overcome wakefulness is disturbed by the snoring of John. In another instance, the two are closely paralleled when each, independently, watches part of the same television show in their

Figures 10 and 11 Parallels established at the extra-diegetic level: Charlotte and Bob watching TV in their hotel beds. © 2003 Universal Studios

hotel bedroom (although we first see Bob switching channels to a pro-gramme different from that seen in Charlotte's room, a sound overlap to the image of Bob wielding his remote indicates that the preceding shot of the television tuned to the station viewed by Charlotte is the one in his room rather than hers).

Correspondences between the two created in this manner occupy an extra-diegetic realm, imposed through montage juxtaposition, to which are added a developing series of diegetic meetings, starting with momen-tarily shared glances and a smile from Charlotte in an elevator (an initial point of contact she later seems not to recall). The principal arena in which the relationship between the characters is initially developed is the hotel bar, in which their mutual belonging is again emphasised through separation from others indicated either by late-night insomniac hours or distinction between what is marked as the privileged contact they establish and the 'superficial' pop-culture world associated with John: initially, a mutual exchange of smiles and the sending over of a dish of olives by Charlotte, in a sequence in which she is distanced from John and the rock band associates with whom they share a table. This is followed by the first real exchange between Bob and Charlotte during one of the late-night assignations. Subsequent examples include an occasion on which Charlotte escapes the irksome chatter of another of John's acquaintances, the Hollywood starlet Kelly, a figure who acts as a strong marker of the cultural distinctions drawn within the film, to whom we return below.

In the latter of these examples Bob quips to Charlotte that he is 'trying to organise a prison break' and is looking for 'an accomplice', a comment that indicates another characteristic dimension of romantic comedy embraced by the film: the 'escape' of the central couple or couple-to-be and their enjoyment of a realm figured as one of 'play' and distinguished from what is presented as the imprisoning world of everyday routine. Bob subsequently joins Charlotte in a night out with a group of Japanese friends, a bonding experience marked as one of freedom and more genuine contact with aspects of the local culture than anything that has gone before. They socialise in a club and the impression of escape is repeated when an altercation on the part of one of their companions results in the group being chased out into the street under fire from a BB gun, increasing the sense of exhilaration resulting from shared fun, play, adventure and freedom from formally restrained behaviour. This is a quintessential ingredient of many classic romantic comedies, in which 'stuffy' characters often find love after being inducted into the world of play or other sources of freedom from what is characterised as excessive social constraint.[28] A similar impression is created in an escape into the streets by Bob and Charlotte from the inappropriate surroundings of a sex bar, the location in which they arrange to meet the same group of friends on a subsequent night, a sequence that ends back in the hotel where the pair laugh conspiratorially (a further indication of bonding) while avoiding contact with an embarrassing singing performance by Kelly. A sense of wry humour and play in fact characterises the couple's exchanges from the start, including some of the sequences considered in the first part of this chapter.

It is also possible to read into *Lost in Translation* a related thematic opposition between the two central characters, another standard feature of many examples of romantic comedy. Different personal qualities are often projected onto each half of the central couple, to be given a kind of magical resolution that accompanies the eventual union of the individuals. A classic version, as suggested above, is that one stands for a world of fun, play and irresponsibility while the other is a representative of more 'serious' or stuffy qualities. The latter is usually subject to the greatest transformation, in the name of 'love', but such exchanges can also involve varying degrees to which each is presented as learning from the other in the crafting of a more balanced position. In *Lost in Translation*, Bob is cast to a large extent as the 'joker', as manifested in some of the more performative routines considered earlier in this chapter and in his proposal of the notion of 'escape' from the hotel with Charlotte (even if it is she who later makes the concrete invitation to go out with her friends). The latter is, in general, the more studious, critical and introverted of the pair (she describes herself as 'so mean' and Bob comments on her reluctance to smile) and does appear to be 'opened up' to some extent as a result of her adventures with Bob (although this is qualified, as are other more generic aspects of the film, by the fact that Coppola gives what is presented as serious weight and substance to the position of both protagonists, manifested in the case of Bob in the more 'sincere' dimensions of characterisation and performance detailed above).

Where *Lost in Translation* most clearly departs from romantic comedy convention is the direction in which all of this is leading, which is not towards sexual consummation, its promise or necessarily romance as such at all. The movement might appear to be in this direction, both generally and in some specific instances, especially in the exchange between the principals that follows the escape from the sex bar. Charlotte is awake and restless later that night and an invitation from Bob is slid under her door. The characters join up in his room for their most intimate experience in the film, as analysed above, the sequence in which they end up sitting and lying together on the bed and engaged in a serious discussion of personal issues in their lives. A 'magical' quality of the kind often found in romantic comedy is given to one moment, when the image of the seated pair is viewed as a reflection in the window, superimposed upon a night sky filled with the lights of the city. Subsequently, they lie side-by-side but remain fully clothed. At one point they turn to face each other, in increased intimacy, but physical contact is restricted to the placing of

Bob's hand on Charlotte's foot, at which point the image fades to black (implying that they go to much-needed sleep, rather than an ellipsis during which any further physical contact occurs). Any expectation of a sexual turn to the relationship is quashed, displaced in effect, it might be argued, onto a subsequent one-night stand between Bob and the hotel lounge singer (Catherine Lambert), an event that drives a wedge briefly between Bob and Charlotte. This is another movement that might be associated with the conventions of romantic comedy: a foolish wrong step that threatens to destroy the couple but is ultimately either averted or repaired. The nature of the central relationship is presented as increasingly close friendship more than romance, however, and friendship that remains friendship rather than eventually becoming transformed into romance, as might more conventionally be anticipated.[29] The more seriously coded doubts and questions raised during Bob and Charlotte's most sustained conversations, especially the sequence on the bed, retain their weight to a greater extent than is customary in even the more questioning examples of Hollywood romantic comedy, in which the central romantic ideal tends to be sustained even where some space is given to acknowledgment of its status as myth.

Lost in Translation ultimately defies the expectations of the 'May–September' variety of romance or romantic comedy, in which younger and older partners are united (the former, in patriarchal currency, usually the woman, the latter the man). Key signifiers of the genre continue to be drawn upon in the closing scenes, however, in the final stages of parting. The relationship is re-established after Bob's sexual dalliance when the two meet in what seems to be another privileged space, outside the hotel at night during a fire-alarm evacuation, after which they repair once more to the bar. They kiss briefly in an elevator when they separate for the rest of the night. On the final morning, Bob tries to ring Charlotte in her room, but fails to make contact, creating a moment of tension (will he, and by extension the viewer, be denied a more satisfactory parting?). She appears in the lobby, as he is about to leave, and they part in a sequence that is brief, awkward and does not appear to provide an adequate resolution to the relationship developed throughout the film, largely because they are not alone or in the kind of company that has allowed them to express themselves more honestly, Bob being accompanied here by a group of hotel personnel and having just diverted the attentions of a woman fan. As Bob is driven away to the airport he glimpses a figure in the crowd, instructs his driver to wait and catches up with Charlotte on the street, in what appears to be a classic transformative romantic comedy moment, the cue usually for a last-minute all-out declaration of love and the imposition of romantic closure, returning to the 'alone in a crowd' status that has marked some privileged moments earlier in the piece. They enter a sustained embrace and he speaks into her ear, although the words are rendered deliberately inaudible to the viewer. This is followed by a full kiss on the lips and what is more clearly marked as an emotionally satisfying final parting. Whether the two are destined to remain with their existing partners or whether the relationship between Bob and Charlotte will continue in some form, romantic or otherwise, is left at least to some extent open, a device through which Coppola is able to maintain a balance between use of and departure from more familiar generic convention.

In form, the series of tension-building delayed-ending moves that leads to the climax seems to abide by the generic pattern, although in content it is by several degrees distinct, based largely on the different nature of the relationship that has been established within the central couple. Any impression of an ongoing connection between the two is not sufficient to outweigh a real sense of a parting that seems, eventually, mostly likely to be definitive. At this point in the narrative the dominant expectation generated by the film is likely to be for the conventional romantic happy ending to be avoided rather than fulfilled as the latter would be too sharp and late a turn towards wholesale adoption of mainstream convention to seem probable, on the basis of the trajectory established up to that moment. This is a crucial factor in the broader positioning of the film as an indie or Indiewood product, the credentials of which might be viewed as making it close to impossible for the film suddenly to have veered in the direction of entirely straightforward romantic conformity. In place of the emotional release and resolution more typical of the mainstream variety, *Lost in Translation* evokes a general impression of longing that is some way short of being fulfilled at the end, although some of the resonances of emotional resolution are provided by the multi-stage manner in which the parting is deployed. The maintenance of something closer to mainstream dynamics in form is an effective manner in which to produce some of the conventional pay-off, in a broad sense of seeming to do justice to the work that has gone into the development of the relationship, while maintaining a marked degree of distinction at the level of the actual detail of the events.

The nature of its employment of devices familiar from romantic comedy is another manifestation of the particular positioning of the film in the wider cultural spectrum. Some more mainstream/Hollywood romantic comedies also mix comic-romantic and more serious resonances, sometimes venturing into territory associated with romantic melodrama.[30] An attempt is made in numerous films of recent decades to 'have it both ways', to acknowledge the mythical nature of the romantic ideal and to admit some of the less reconcilable dimensions of contemporary life/relationships, but also to re-enact the mythic outcome more or less intact.[31] The position of *Lost in Translation* is closer to that of a number of varieties of romantic comedy found in the indie or Indiewood sectors that offer more substantial twists on the generic routine, although the extent of departure varies considerably from one example to another.[32] As far as a broad sense of the identity of the film is concerned at the textual level, romantic comedy does appear to be a substantial component, alongside the presence of the star/s and the auteur factor, but in a manner that seems, essentially, to be qualified. If *Lost in Translation* is not 'just' or 'simply' a romantic comedy – or not 'really' a romantic comedy as such at all – it seems that the 'not' is italicised and emphasised. *Not* a romantic comedy can be understood as a positive rather than merely negative signifier for a film marked quite conspicuously by the extent to which – despite its mobilisations of some core generic devices – it denies any full belonging to the genre as a key aspect of its claim to a more distinctive position.

The category 'romantic comedy' is employed by strikingly few of the Amazon reviewers, however, even if the majority of these understand the film as an example that departs from the usual conventions of the genre. A total of just thirty-two out of 1,900 use the term (1.6 per cent). Of these only three locate the film straightforwardly in the category (0.15 per cent) while twenty (just over 1 per cent) overtly suggest that it represents an unconventional variety of the format. Genre categories of any kind are used significantly less than those relating to the star or filmmaker, and in a more fragmented manner, which might say as much about the hybrid nature of the film as it does about the deployment of genre as a discursive category more generally by filmgoers. *Lost in Translation* is understood in some relationship to comedy or humour by 320 respondents (16.8 per cent), considerably fewer than those who make reference to Murray or Coppola as points of orientation. Of these, 101 (5.3 per cent of the sample or 31.5 per cent of those who make reference to comedy/humour) complain about a lack of comedy in the film, either generally or in response to how they suggest the film has been marketed or labelled by others: 'If it was supposed to be a comedy, it failed because I didn't laugh once', as one puts it (William, Florida, 24 February 2004).

Some form of broadly 'straight' or conventional comic enjoyment is found in the film by 129 (6.7 per cent overall or 40 per cent of those referring to comedy/humour), either as a broad dimension of judgement of the film ('hysterically funny', Karen A. Lynch, 11 January 2007) or, for many, only in parts ('This movie moves at a snail pace but it still has its funny moments', A Customer 28 March 2004). Some such comments are specifically related to Murray's performance but far from all. Considerably more express what appears to be a broadly conventional variety of comic pleasure than the number who make specific reference to less mainstream or more subtle forms of comedy, which suggests that the film was able to cross over to a wider form of appeal for some viewers in this dimension, although those who directly express such a response remain a small minority of the total sample. Comments relating to qualities such as 'subtle', 'understated', 'dry' or 'dark' humour, mostly positive, are made by fifty-five respondents (2.8 per cent of the total or 17 per cent of those who refer to the comic dimension in general). Many also comment on the fact that *Lost in Translation* is not 'really' or not 'just' a comedy, but that it mixes comedy and other dimensions such as 'drama' or 'tragedy'. As one puts it, the film 'runs the line between quiet humour and introspective melancholy' (D. Pawl, Seattle, 21 January 2007).

That terms of generic identification are employed relatively infrequently in these responses is further demonstrated by the use of labels referring to the romantic dimension of the film. A total of sixty refer to *Lost in Translation* as a 'romance' or a 'love story' (3.15 per cent of the sample). Twenty-two of these use the terms more or less straightforwardly, usually in passing, while thirty-eight highlight the unconventional take on the format employed by Coppola. As one of the latter puts it: 'Those expecting a May-December love story are watching the wrong film' (Josh Hitchens, Philadelphia, PA, 9 August 2004), while another terms it 'a beautiful almost-romance' (Melissa Niksic, Chicago, IL United States, 19 April 2005). Many of the reviewers who respond most positively to the film comment on its emotional power, whether or not this is put in terms of its use of or departure from more conventional forms of romance or romantic comedy. It is only a small minority, however, who articulate this in terms of the precise nature of the relationship between the film and romantic comedy, as in the following: 'No stereotypes, no clichés, and by no means the standard romantic comedy formula is used in any way to cheapen the carefully constructed atmosphere of lonesome existences and frailty of the soul' (Adrian Duran Sanchez, Costa Rica, 2 November 2004).

While many respondents avoid generic indicators altogether, the number who focus specifically on the subject of genre or category as such is very small. Just nine reviews comment directly on the fact that the film does not easily fit into any genre categories. As one of these puts it:

It's a movie that kind of defies categorization: it's not really a romance, it's sure not an action thriller or a mystery or sci-fi or fantasy or horror. So what is it? I think Lost in Translation is a visual essay on the modern condition. (Peggy Vincent, Oakland, CA, 25 February 2004)

It may be precisely for this reason – that it does not easily fit into any single category – that the majority of reviews avoid genre or other such category labels altogether. Genre is, arguably, a dimension most likely to become a point of reference where it is most clearly in evidence, either in conventional form or where its parameters are most explicitly undermined or transgressed. While the above example is part of a positive evaluation of *Lost in Translation*, criticism is also expressed in some cases in terms of the absence of clear-cut genre components, including but not restricted to the absence of comedy. 'This film doesn't even have a genre', complains one respondent in evident disgust at a work declared to be 'possibly one of the worst movies I've ever seen' (A Customer, 10 April 2004). For others, 'it is not romantic and it is most certainly not funny' (Terselax, 3 January 2007) or 'The movie is not funny, and it is not dramatic. What it is is a waste of time' (Rusty, Fremont, CA United States, 8 August 2004). A clear dividing line seems to exist between those who appreciate and take pleasure from the perception that the film is not restricted to the specific confines of particular genres or modalities such as comedy and drama and those from whom this is a source of displeasure and a ground for rejection. On the whole, though, if the film draws upon elements associated with romantic comedy in some key structural mechanisms, as suggested above, this is not generally acknowledged by the Amazon reviewers.

Lost in Translation can also be located in relation to a number of individual films with which it shares certain qualities, both within and beyond the boundaries of romantic comedy. Probably the most obvious point of reference from the independent sector is Richard Linklater's

Before Sunrise (1994), an account of a day and night spent together by a young couple who meet on a train. It shares with *Lost in Translation* an open stance on the possibility of a future relationship between the two, who initially agree to make no further contact but eventually arrange to meet again six months later, an explicit negotiation of their situation that is largely absent from Coppola's film. *Before Sunrise* also mixes the employment and undercutting of romantic conventions: its setting in Vienna, broadly and in the specific detail of a number of scenes, plays up the romantic dimension while the discussions between the protagonists that constitute the bulk of the fabric of the film are more critically interrogative of concepts such as love, romance and the institution of marriage; there is also conventional sexually oriented romance, in that the pair exchange passionate kisses and eventually make love in a city park. From a very different historical context, the final parting in *Lost in Translation* has been compared with that of the classic stiff-upper-lip British romance, *Brief Encounter* (1945).

Another reference point employed by some critics, in relation to aspects of its central relationship and its broader atmospheric texture, is Wong Kar Wai's *In the Mood for Love* (*Fa yeung nin wa*, Hong Kong, 2000), which traces the friendship that develops between a couple whose spouses prove to be having an affair, building towards a state of unfulfilled yearning after their separation. The same cinematographer was employed on *In the Mood for Love* and an additional overseas film that became a point of comparison, released in the US the year after *Lost in Translation*, the Japan/Thailand co-production *Last Life in the Universe* (*Ruang rak noi nid mhasan*, 2003), another moody piece, in this case increasingly oblique and elusive, the focus of which is the relationship between an obsessive-compulsive suicidal Japanese man and a young Thai woman.[33] From the point of view of both marketing and reviewing, connections of these kinds between individual films are often stressed as much as or more than genre locations, the successful status of *Lost in Translation* being such that it became itself a reference point – a translation into more familiar terms – for some subsequent features, particularly for overseas productions that might otherwise be harder to sell outside their regions of origin. A review quotation used prominently on the region 2 DVD cover of *Last Life in the Universe* refers to it as 'One of Asia's milestone films . . . Casts as compelling a lovelorn spell as *Lost in Translation*', while Yang Zimou's *Riding Alone for Thousands of Miles* (*Qian li zou dan qi*, 2005) was described in one trade review as 'a Chinese "Lost in Translation".'[34]

Some of these individual films are also used as reference points within the Amazon sample, but they are found amid a very wide plurality of others. Wong Kar Wai receives the largest number of citations, fifteen, either by name or in reference to *In the Mood for Love* or some of his other work. *Before Sunrise* is cited by only two. The most heavily cited other features are *American Beauty* (1999) with twelve and *About Schmidt* (2002) with nine, each of which is similarly located in indie/Indiewood territory. As with many other examples, such films are used both positively and negatively, depending on the orientation of the viewer (that is to say, as other examples of qualities found in *Lost in Translation* that are either celebrated or condemned). *Brief Encounter* features with six citations and *Eternal Sunshine of the Spotless Mind* with seven. One of the other most referenced titles is the television series *Seinfeld* (1989–98), on the basis of its status of being a series 'about nothing' (again, used as a reference point from both positive and negative perspectives), a territory that leads some reviewers into references to representatives of international art cinema including Francois Truffaut, Jean-Luc Godard, Michelangelo Antonioni (a perhaps somewhat surprising eight references), Ingmar Bergman and Andrei Tarkovsky, along with movements such as Italian neorealism and the French *nouvelle vague*. These and the names of other filmmakers such as David Lynch, Wim Wenders, Jim Jarmusch and Wayne Wang are also mixed with literary reference points including James Joyce, Ernest Hemingway and Haruki Murakami.

If *Lost in Translation* is positioned in a particular manner in relation to both genre and other individual films, filmmakers or authors, markers of a broader cinematic kind are also found within the diegesis, particularly in relation to the character of Kelly, the Hollywood actress cited above. Kelly is a former acquaintance of John, in Tokyo to promote her latest film, 'Midnight Velocity', a martial-arts-oriented action movie supposedly starring Keanu Reeves. The film-within-the-film, and its representative, Kelly, function quite plainly as marker points, standing for the kind of cinema – and culture, more broadly – against which *Lost in Translation* seems intended to be defined. Kelly is presented as crass, shallow and annoying, personal qualities that Coppola's film appears to associate with a wider realm of popular cinema. When the gushing, breathless 'airhead' is first introduced to Charlotte, the viewer is invited to share the latter's disparaging response (Charlotte looks Kelly up and down, as if subjecting her to critical inspection). As Kelly and John converse, part of the exchange is framed with one on each side of the

Figure 12 Critical inspection: the viewer invited to share Charlotte's disparaging look at Kelly. © 2003 Universal Studios

screen and Charlotte in between, facing them but also turned towards the camera, emphasising her unimpressed response more than their dialogue itself. A strong sense is created of seeking to align the viewer with her position, even if some might agree with John's comment at the end of the sequence about her tendency to highlight the stupidity of others ('not everybody went to Yale') in relation to her amused reaction to the fact that Kelly is using the pseudonym 'Evelyn Waugh' without realising that it was the name of a man.

Kelly's 'crassness', as a negative pole of distinction in the dynamics of *Lost in Translation*, is later underlined in a sequence in which Charlotte observes her performance in part of a 'Midnight Velocity' press conference in the hotel and in the singing scene cited above. The world of Kelly and 'Midnight Velocity' is presented as one from which Bob has become alienated, his stardom being owed primarily, it seems, to his own earlier performances in action films (the equivalent, it seems, of Murray's origins in broad comedy). If such work, and the ultimate sell-out represented by his whisky endorsements, is juxtaposed with the notion of 'doing a play somewhere', at a 'higher' and more 'worthwhile' cultural level, much the same kind of opposition is implied between the 'lower' reaches of the commercial cinema mainstream – of which the action film is often taken as representative – and the kind of status sought by the likes of *Lost in Translation*. It seems no accident that the film enjoyed by Bob and Charlotte in the privileged hotel bedroom sequence, Federico Fellini's *La*

Dolce Vita, is a certified work of international art cinema, one with which Coppola's film shares some thematic dimensions.[35]

This kind of broader cultural distinction-marking and position-taking occurs very prominently in a substantial proportion of the Amazon responses, both in general and in reference to specific qualities of the film. A frequent strategy among those who express a positive opinion is to compare *Lost in Translation* favourably with more mainstream Hollywood productions, among which action films loom especially large as a signifier of undemanding mainstream fare (the action film, as a negative point of reference, is cited as frequently as the genres within which the film might at least partly be located). Such acts of distinction-marking in relation to the film tend to have quite clear implications at the level of what is suggested about the viewer. In order for the film to be appreciated, it is implied, certain kinds of personal qualities are required, sometimes expressed positively but often in terms of their opposite or absence in others. What is involved here is the mobilisation of particular resources of cultural capital, as defined by Pierre Bourdieu (a learned ability to appreciate or take pleasure from particular forms of cultural production), an issue to which we return in the consideration of the formal dimensions of the film in the following chapter.

Distinction-marking articulations of one kind or another are made by 299 respondents in the sample of 1,900 (15.5 per cent), the majority offering more or less explicit statements about the kinds of viewers considered likely to 'get' the film (269: 14 per cent of the total or 89.6 per cent of those engaging in such comparisons). Some rise little above the level of personal insult, establishing their own position through negative reference. 'If you don't get this movie, UR dumb!', as one puts it (Bodega Noriega, Brooklyn, 10 November 2006), while for another, typical of many of this kind, the film is 'Not for the dim-witted' (MrQ, USA, 4 September 2007). Others focus on the positive qualities they consider to be required for appreciation of the film: 'This is very much a thinking person's film' (James Sadler, Garland, TX United States, 13 April 2004); 'Anyone with any depth should feel compelled by this film, even if they don't fall in love with it like I did' (J. Merrill, Georgia, 11 November 2007); 'if you can handle a movie that runs this deep, go swimming!' (Jordan 'green eyed kat', Atlanta, GA USA, 28 June 2005). Other typical responses adopt an 'if/but' formulation that occurs quite frequently in such articulations in relation to this and other films,[36] as in the following examples. 'If you're expecting an action-packed drama or quirky romantic comedy, you'll be horribly disappointed. But if you're looking for a beautiful and deep look at love and romance, give this movie a go' (Aaron Hildebrandt, Canada, 28 April 2004). 'If you're looking for an action movie with its share of sex and violence, this isn't it, but if your [sic] looking for great entertainment that also leaves you thinking, this is the one you want' (A Customer, 1 February 2004).

Some respondents take a more balanced or neutral approach to the suggestion that the film might be suited to certain tastes rather than others, but these are very much in the minority (twenty-five, or 8.3 per cent of those who engage in these issues). Nearly twice as many (forty-nine, or 16.4 per cent of those who enter this debate) mount what can be seen as a counter-offensive against those who make either personal or sweeping attacks on those perceived not to 'get' the film because of their intellectual ability or other individual or collective qualities. For some of these, it is a matter simply of throwing insults in the opposite direction ('this is a pathetic movie with pathetic characters for pathetic moviegoers', George Hale, San Antonio, TX USA, 2 September 2004), but many make more pointed criticism of what they see as the 'pretentious' character of either all of those who admire the film or those who use it to make overt points of distinction of the kind cited above. 'This is the type of movie where all the ARTSY freaks come out to describe just how brilliant it is', as one suggests (tyson 'nothing man', Dover, NJ United States, 21 July 2004), while another opens with: 'If you are a pseudo-intellectual, this is your film' ('chuckpatrick', NJ, 5 June 2004).

Some of those who dislike the film question the polarised terms of debate used by many of its admirers, rejecting the simple opposition between films of this kind and the negative pole provided by various notions of the 'dumb' action movie, 'crude' comedy or effects-led Hollywood blockbuster. 'There may be many moments of slow-paced dialogue', suggests one, 'but just because slow-paced dialogue is in direct contrast to flashy cutting and exploding cars does not automatically make characters and themes complex' (canticles, San Francisco, CA USA, 13 May 2005). Another appends a 'note' to the end of a posting that reads:

To the stuck-up 5-star reviews who think that the only people who hate this movie are braindead jocks who only like movies like xXx and The Fast and the Furious . . . do us a favor and shut the hell up. I like artsy, intellectual movies as much as the next guy, but Lost In Translation just flat-out isn't as deep as some people make it out to be. (Kazuo, 8 July 2005)

Several others follow suit, emphasising their general appreciation of independent or 'art-house' films in an attempt to undermine the binary logic imposed by some, an additional example reading as follows:

I'm a big fan of the so-called 'Intelligent movies', movies that challenge Hollywood established pattern of stupid action, CGI stupid effects, plot holes wider than a football stadium. But to see a pile of crap like this get so much praise really annoys me. (Gergellor, Superimpalândia, 6 October 2004)

A few try to lower the temperature of such exchanges, which do become heated and personal at times. As one suggests:

I think it takes a certain type of personality to relate to a movie like this but it's certainly nothing to be bitter about. I've read posts where the people rating the movie as a 1 star personally attack anyone that dares enjoy the film. That's a shame. We all have different tastes and some are more complex (or weird if that makes you happy) than others and there's no need to try and insult someone over a difference in opinion. (J. Ensley, Richmond, VA, 1 August 2004)

The strength of feeling expressed in many of these responses can be taken as evidence of significant degrees of investment for some viewers in what their tastes and preferences are perceived to say about broader aspects of their character or their socio-cultural location, and about the role that can be played by films such as *Lost in Translation* in the articulation of such discourses. The process of distinction-marking that unfolds within the text is mirrored in a significant number of viewer responses, although the latter is a far less one-way process, reflecting the more varied disposition that exists among a sample as apparently widely drawn as that provided by Amazon reviews.

3. Form: Narrative, Visual Style, Music

Narrative: the attenuation of 'classical' form

The narrative dimension is one in which *Lost in Translation* is most clearly marked as a product of the indie sector, its primary defining feature being its comparative slightness. *Lost in Translation* is a production in which, by mainstream standards, relatively little happens. Plotting is restricted largely to the development of the relationship between Bob and Charlotte, a relationship that itself, as seen in the previous chapter, refuses to conform to more conventional 'romantic' expectations, despite the employment of certain devices familiar from the template of romantic comedy. *Lost in Translation* fits, in this respect, into a wider tendency, particularly at the lower-budget end of the indie sector, towards the use of downplayed narrative frameworks. These stand in contrast to both the heightened worlds, plot-points and arcs typical of the Hollywood mainstream and the more complex narrative structures favoured by certain other strains of independent production.[1] The downplayed version can in some examples be understood as a more or less direct response to practical/financial limitations, scenarios of this variety generally requiring fewer resources. It can also be a strategy more central to the creative logic of the work, however, as seems clearly to be the case in this instance.

If *Lost in Translation* exhibits a 'reduced' narrative format, focused on the unfolding of the Bob/Charlotte relationship, it also retains much in common with the more conventional/mainstream 'classical' Hollywood version, as is the case with many indie features. Key dimensions of the classical form employed by the film include its focus on a specifically defined period in the lives of a small number of central individual characters; its temporal division into a clearly established beginning, middle and end; and its use of a clearly comprehensible cause/effect logic, in which one development leads to and/or is explained by another. The film opens with what appears to be a narratively unlocated image, of Charlotte's bottom, as she lies on a bed in transparent pink underwear, as examined at the start of this book, but quite quickly moves to establish context. Credits over this image are followed by a black screen and the main title, behind which we hear the sound of an airplane and the announcement of an arrival at Tokyo's Narita airport. An 'arrival' of this kind is a familiar and entirely conventional narrative starting point, reinforced in the following sequence in which a drowsing Bob awakes in a car – assumed to be taking him from the airport. Shots of the neon cityscape emphasise the arrival at a new and 'exotic' location, as does the greeting received by Bob at the Park Hyatt. The nature of his reception also establishes that Bob is a notable figure of some kind, the basis of his fame being explained shortly afterwards by two young businessmen who seek to engage him in conversation in the hotel bar in another device symptomatic of the classical style. The existence of some degree of tension in his domestic life is indicated, with typically classical narrative economy, through the receipt of a fax from home in which he is informed that he forgot his son's birthday. A good deal of background information is 'effortlessly' conveyed in this manner, worked into the detail of the opening scenes rather than being given more overt explication. Charlotte is introduced in full in the first of the several juxtapositions cited in the previous chapter, sitting in her hotel room window, unable to sleep.

The first half-hour or so of the film is devoted to the further establishment of each character, their reasons for being in Tokyo and the creation of additional juxtapositions. Broad classical/mainstream convention creates a strong expectation that the paths of the two will cross, their status as the principals having been made clear, even without the overt acts of juxtaposition detailed in the previous chapter.[2] If Charlotte is already at the hotel at the start of the film – if we locate the opening image in time, rather than treating it as more free-floating – the arrival of Bob might be understood as beginning a process of coming to join her, specifically, rather than just to the hotel in general. Their first contact (the brief sharing of glances in the lift) occurs eight minutes into the film, more sustained eye-contact (the sequence in the bar in which Charlotte sends a dish of olives over to Bob) coming at the 24-minute mark.[3] The first part of *Lost in Translation* can be understood as conforming to a standard opening-act structure, the classical tradition usually being associated with either a three- or four-act composition (opening act, complicating longer middle act and shorter final act in the three-act version, the middle act being divided into two in readings that divide features into four acts).[4] The end of the first act of the film might be identified as the point at which the two principals first engage in a proper, sustained conversation at night in the bar, a sequence that begins around the 31-minute mark. At this stage they have each been introduced in some detail, some parallels in their situations have been suggested and these now begin to bear fruit in the beginning of a more sustained relationship. As an opening act, this is relatively long for a film that runs to approximately ninety-six minutes (not including end credits), the conventional template usually being considered to display a relationship of approximately 1-2-1 between the three acts (or 1-1-1-1 in the four-act rendition), according to which the first act of *Lost in Translation* would be expected to last closer to twenty-four minutes (the timing, as it happens, of that first contact in the bar, a moment that in itself seem too passing clearly to mark the end of the initial movement of juxtapositions and early connections). This is indicative of the leisurely pacing of the film and the greater than usual time it spends in bringing its two principals 'properly' together.

From this point, the main body of the film is devoted to tracing the gradual development of the relationship through the various stages outlined in the genre section of the previous chapter. In the conventional Hollywood recipe, a number of 'complicating' events, obstacles and sources of antagonism would be expected, plot devices that delay the achievement by the central protagonist/s of their major goals. This is the case to only a limited extent in *Lost in Translation*. It seems clear that the relationship itself reaches its peak in the sequence during which Bob and Charlotte share heartfelt exchanges in his bedroom, following the second of their two 'escapes' from the confines of the hotel (and, by implication, from the restraints created by their respective domestic and broader 'life' situations). This appears to end with a resolution to the question of whether or not their relationship is to move in a sexual direction: if that did not happen in this instance, with so many indicators in place of movement towards closer intimacy, it seems unlikely to happen thereafter, leaving the relationship quite firmly established as one of close friendship rather than anything more explicitly 'romantic' in nature. This sequence finishes at about the 73-minute mark, but does not appear to indicate the closing of a clearly defined middle-act sequence, being followed by further scenes devoted to the separate actions of the two characters (including Charlotte's visit to Kyoto and Bob's TV talk-show appearance). The closest the film comes to a narrative/dramatic crisis is revealed at eighty-two minutes, when we (closely followed by Charlotte) discover that Bob has slept with the lounge singer, although this appears to have been resolved within less than four minutes, when the characters 'make up' during the fire-alarm evacuation. This seems typical of the generally attenuated, low-key nature of much of the narrative material of the film. The final act might be what follows from here, lasting some ten minutes, during which the substantial nature of the attraction shared by the pair is underlined (he tells her he does not want to leave, to which she replies 'don't; stay here with me', although she undercuts this with a joke about them starting a jazz band) but their parting also becomes inevitable.

If *Lost in Translation* can be fitted into something like a three-act structure, the above analysis suggests that it might do so only up to a point. A reasonably clear first act can be identified, as can a relatively brief final act, but it is not the case that this kind of structural breakdown is most pertinent to the overall effect created by the film. A broader pattern of parallels, juxtapositions, meetings, shared and separate experiences by the two protagonists seems to apply across the length of the running time. There are clear elements of progression in the way these function in some respects, for example the manner in which initially separate experiences are combined with juxtapositions and a developing series of meetings/engagements between the two. But this is not a process that moves anything like entirely in a direction of integration. Bob and Charlotte continue to occupy their own, sometimes separate spaces even towards the end of the film. *Lost in Translation* continues to obey a logic that is partly episodic – as found in some 'classic' examples of indie cinema, including *Slacker* (1991) and *Clerks* (1994) – as well as building its episodes into a more progressive/cumulative dynamic. But there is a balance between the two. Elements that might at first appear narratively more arbitrary or episodic are often tied in, more or less significantly, to ongoing developments of one kind or another. Two examples are provided by sequences that follow the comic routine involving Bob on the exercise bicycle and another in which he swims in the hotel pool, accompanied by a group taking part in an aerobic routine.

The exercise bike scene is rather arbitrary and free-standing, as suggested in the previous chapter. It is tied into the following sequence, however, according to a basic logic of cause/effect, even if this is not of great significance in itself: we see Bob on what is assumed to be the next day, walking stiffly as a result of the ordeal, as he meets hotel staff in the lobby. This is just a passing and oblique link, a moment of low-key humour, but it provides connecting tissue between the comic routine and what will become a more significant narrative thread. Bob's scene with the hotel staff is followed (and joined via a dialogue overlap) by Charlotte and John walking in a similar direction, away from camera and towards lighted doors or windows, into another hotel space (which might at first be taken to be another part of the same lobby, although it appears subsequently to be on a higher floor) where they bump into Kelly at the start of what develops into an important strand (Kelly, as we have seen, functioning as both a marker point in the positioning of the film and a narrative device through which Charlotte is pushed closer to Bob). The swimming-pool sequence is, likewise, drawn into what becomes part of an important ongoing dynamic. At first, it is just Bob undergoing a further experience that includes a measure of bemusement at the activities by which he is surrounded. It soon becomes another marker of parallelism within the couple, however. Charlotte is also seen in the pool, a few scenes later, and the paths of the pair cross in a corridor, he on his way for a swim, as she heads back to her room afterwards – and it is at this point that she invites him to join her and her friends for their narratively important night out in the city.

Elements such as these are the entirely normal, even banal, stuff of carefully constructed narrative sequence of a variety that is broadly classical in its detail. If the episodic quality often seems to the fore, this is partly a matter of the pacing of individual sequences that are very often leisurely and dedicated to the establishment or development of mood and atmospherics as much as narrative or thematic resonances (although these are far from always separable elements). The unhurried nature of the film does not make it non-linear, but it does in many cases reduce the sense of priority given to linearity, to the direct linking of actions or events from one sequence to another. This is another quite clear marker of indie status. More time is taken to evoke the impressions, feelings and experiences of the central characters than would be expected to be found in a mainstream Hollywood film, often in sequences that in themselves contribute little if anything to linear narrative development. One example of this is the sequence in which Charlotte takes a trip to Kyoto, immediately following the narrative high point of the 'heartfelt' encounter in Bob's hotel room.

It might be conventional to follow a heightened sequence with one that is quieter and more leisurely, as a form of relief, creating an impression of light-and-shade, but the Kyoto scenes are more extended than would be necessary to fulfil any such purpose. From the black screen ending the previous sequence, we open on a landscape vista featuring a snow-topped mountain, followed by shots of Charlotte looking out of a bullet train window, further shots of the passing view and her arrival at Kyoto station. In Kyoto, she visits a temple, wanders the gardens and observes a passing wedding party before adding her own contribution to a shrine comprised of twists of paper. The sequence is wordless, lasting just under three minutes, and is one of a number of elements of 'local colour' experience that could easily be removed from the film without notice as far as overt plot development is concerned. It is followed by a series of scenes involving Bob, without Charlotte: attempting to shave with a tiny complimentary razor; sneaking out of the hotel to avoid the attentions of its staff; reacting with typical bemusement to the spectacle created by a passing campaign bus of some variety; running across a multi-lane road; making a call on his mobile phone to agree to appear in the talk show for which he has been asked to delay his departure from Tokyo; appearing on the show; looking at a picture of Charlotte taken during their night out with her Japanese friends; in a bath at the hotel where he takes a phone call from his wife in which he talks about his desire to 'get healthy' and to eat better, a conversation that includes intimations of both problems with and remaining potential in their relationship; taking a sauna, in the company of two Germans; watching part of his TV appearance and switching off; and then meeting the hotel singer at the bar and waking up to find her in his room the following morning. Some of this is relevant to the status of the Bob/Charlotte relationship, in the aftermath of their most intimate exchange – his examination of the photograph, his conversation with his wife, the dalliance with the singer – but most of it is not. Much of the emphasis of this and Charlotte's Kyoto sequence is on mood, atmosphere and the development of thematic resonances – responses to 'alienating' aspects of Japanese culture – rather than ongoing narrative progression. The gap between the end of the bedroom sequence and the 'crisis' generated by the revelation of Bob's night with the singer is some nine minutes, a substantial interval for this stage of the film, which suggests that its investment is not solely in the one major plot thread that traces the development of their relationship.

What this amounts to is a shift in the hierarchical arrangement of different elements of the film from what would usually be expected in the majority of mainstream features. The dominant tendency in Hollywood cinema is for plot development to play a stronger role. Character and character relationships remain important in Hollywood films but tend to be deployed and developed to a large extent through the involvement of characters in action and/or other overtly plot-related and heightened elements related to external situations. There are exceptions to this tendency, films in which romance or other interpersonal relations are foregrounded (examples that would often be encompassed by the traditional/stereotypical notion of the 'women's film'), although even here the norm for the mainstream would be for such material to be heightened and driven by romance/relationship-plot more than is the case in *Lost in Translation*. External sources of plot development, in the sense of outside events that intrude strongly upon the fate and experience of the protagonists, are all but absent in Coppola's film, which puts the emphasis on interior experiences to an extent that gives it something in common with the world of art cinema. One external development that might be understood as impacting on the main characters is the request for Bob to remain two extra days in Tokyo in order to appear on the television talk show, providing more time and space for the continuation of his relationship with Charlotte (although this is relatively marginal: if Bob had left on the day originally scheduled he would still have been at the hotel for the night during which the pair share the greatest intimacy; staying longer is what gives him the time to make the 'wrong' move of sleeping with the singer, although it is perhaps their ability to recover from this that indicates some of the substance of the bond between the two). Bob's initial determination not to prolong his stay ('I gotta get out of here, as soon as I can', as he tells his agent on the phone) might appear to establish a more conventional urgency-of-deadline framework, one of the devices typically associated with classical narrative form. But little evidence is shown of any real attempt to achieve this goal, which largely disappears from view until the character seems to drift rather than actively being transformed into a position of going along with the request to delay his departure.

Another plot component of a characteristically minimal but still in itself conventional variety is Charlotte's injury of her toe. This is established relatively early in the film when we see her walk into a table in her hotel room at the 15-minute mark, although it is immediately passed over at the time, any consequence being left entirely in the background. The planting of such an element that will be drawn upon some considerable time later is a standard mainstream narrative ploy. The toe injury becomes an explicit point of reference some forty-five minutes later during conversation between Bob and Charlotte in a sushi bar, leading to his joke routine about 'brack toe' as a Japanese culinary treat, and into the immediately following and mostly comic scenes at the hospital to which he insists on taking her for treatment. It functions as another point of contact, banter and shared experience between the two, motivating the change of scene to the hospital, but it is not a 'development' of any specific plot-related significance in itself (the fact that Charlotte has the injury does not prevent her performance of any action, for example, or initiate any other new narrative development).

While character observation is central to *Lost in Translation*, character is also treated in a more subtle, attenuated manner than is usual in the mainstream. One of the key defining characteristics of classical Hollywood narration (and many other mainstream narrative forms) is a central focus on clearly goal-oriented protagonists, the pursuit of whose goals forms a major part of the narrative armature. Goals can take the form of pre-existing character ambitions or ends created in response to external provocations of various kinds. Bob and Charlotte could be said to have goals, in a broad sense, but not ones that provide narrative-driving action. Each is seeking to 'find' his or her self, to resolve some kind of 'life crisis', but this occurs within an enforced interlude during which little appears to be resolved and certainly not on the basis of active pursuit. Related to this is the question of character development. One of the staples of Hollywood/mainstream oriented screenwriting manuals is a requirement for character development or growth, the tracing out of what has become known as the 'arc' of the major protagonist/s. According to the prescription, characters are meant to be depicted as *learning* from their experiences, overcoming flaws or difficulties. The extent to which this really happens in a substantial manner in Hollywood features is easily exaggerated. It is often a somewhat shallow process, in which qualities that we might already suppose to be latent in central characters (their 'inner' decency, etc.) are merely brought more clearly into the foreground as a result of 'lessons' learnt during the course of the narrative events. Character change of a 'deep seated' nature is 'rarer than we might expect', suggests David Bordwell:

Far more common is character consistency, with the plot being driven by a clash of purposes; gradual character revelation, achieving by delaying the exposition

[. . .]; or character revelation, achieved by thrusting the character into situations that expose different facets of her personality.[5]

Little even of this more modest variety of character change or revelation is found in *Lost in Translation* in relation to either Bob or Charlotte, the characteristics of which seem to remain fairly constant throughout the film. It is implied that each of the principals is beginning to learn something from the other, in their sharing of life experiences. Bob is cast more closely than Charlotte in the position of mentor, especially in the hotel bedroom scenes, offering thoughts based on the longevity of his marriage, although she is also quick to highlight some of the elements of his 'mid-life crisis', particularly in their early exchanges. None of this amounts to a basis for any clear-cut change or enlightenment, however. Little ground is provided in the film for supposing either to have been changed very significantly or in any clearly identifiable, concrete or transforming manner by their shared experiences. This can be understood as one ground for the film's claims to verisimilitude at the narrative level, effectively denying or at least downplaying the (ideologically loaded) implication that the lives of individuals are usually characterised by transformative moments of enlightenment and/or change.

To underline the position of the film in the broader spectrum of narrative options, it is useful to imagine counter-factual possibilities. A film that developed a broadly similar relationship between Bob and Charlotte might be imagined that combined this with more mainstream and generically defined plot dynamics. Such a pair might become embroiled in some kind of crime or thriller plot, for example, in which their relationship were cemented through shared experiences of various forms of action and/or danger. They could become entangled in a drugs or spy-related plot, or be mistaken for criminals and forced on the run. Or, given the plush hotel setting, a disaster-type scenario might be imagined, in which they faced mutual danger of the variety that might be witnessed in an update of *The Towering Inferno* (1974). To propose such alternative scenarios is not merely to indulge in fantasies, but to highlight the particularity of the absence of any such material from the film. Any such presence is conspicuous by its absence, in a manner similar to the way the film can be understood as being defined to some extent specifically as *not* a romantic comedy. The inclusion of minimal elements of material with some distant relation to such phenomena only adds to the marking of distinction. The fact that the group with whom Bob and Charlotte go out for their first night of 'escape' are shot at by a man wielding a BB gun (even a fancy one with some kind of light or laser-based attachment) highlights the absence of any 'real' dangerous action/adventure in *Lost in Translation*, a point that does not seem frivolous given the presence of the action movie as a reference point within the diegesis (in the career backgrounds of both Bob and Kelly). The greatest danger that appears to be faced is that involved in running across busy lanes of city traffic, an activity in which Bob is involved twice and Charlotte once. This minor element of 'action' and 'danger' does play a part in the underlying dynamics of the film, as a marker of moments in which the protagonists engage in forms of escape from their confinement, but its utterly quo-tidian nature is clearly such as to be located a huge distance from the material of the action film. Likewise, the fact that the pair are evacuated from the hotel during a fire alarm is testament to the lack of interest the film has in any such action-adventure, in its conventional forms, their attention and the role of the sequence being devoted to the opportunity the experience offers for the reconfirmation of their friendship.

Counter-factual possibilities could also be imagined in the opposite direction, to emphasise the relatively conventional qualities of the film. If the plotting of *Lost in Translation* is relatively minimal, considerably more minimal scenarios could be envisaged. A version could be imagined in which the two principals only ever experienced passing contact, rather than something that develops, substantially, in its own way, into a more sustained bond. Or two such principals might not make direct contact at all, in a feature that established explicit parallels between them but left them physically apart. Or any connections could be entirely implicit, in a feature that put its emphasis far more strongly on the alienating aspects of the experiences charted by the film. These types of alternative scenario would mark shifts respectively further from the norms of the commercial mainstream, marking perhaps the difference between what convention-ally might be understood as the realms of indie and art cinema, although such distinctions are far from clear-cut. A full understanding of an example such as *Lost in Translation* requires equal attention to both the film's relative difference from the mainstream at the narrative level and its relative similarities when compared with more radical or challenging instances of non-mainstream production.

There are some respects in which *Lost in Translation* might be associ-ated with the conventions of art cinema narration, as defined in ideal-type form by David Bordwell, even if not at the more radical end of the scale.[6] The more episodic structure is one such factor, as is the less goal-oriented nature of the principal characters. For Bordwell, if the protagonist of a Hollywood film can be understood as speeding towards the target, 'the art-film protagonist is presented as sliding passively from one situation to another', a description that seems broadly appropriate to much of *Lost in Translation*, even if the narrative overall is clearer and less prone to gaps than some of the classic instances of art cinema considered by Bordwell.[7] Further: 'If the classical protagonist struggles, the drifting protagonist traces out an itinerary which surveys the social world', a description that seems usefully to capture some of the itineraries traced by the experiences of Bob and Charlotte in Tokyo and Kyoto.[8] Parallelism is also identified by Bordwell as a quality that can come to the fore in art cinema narration, as often seems to be the case in separate sequences featuring the two protagonists of *Lost in Translation*, although this is less a response to a weakening of causal connections than Bordwell suggests is the case in some of his examples. One of the best-known elements of Bordwell's definition of art cinema narration also seems to have substantial purchase on the film. 'Concerned less with action than reaction', he suggests, 'the art cinema presents psychological effects in search of their causes.'[9] This is a useful way to understand the manner in which Bob and Charlotte are presented by Coppola. Each has, in their different way, arrived at a period of crisis that has forced a reconsideration of their life, much of the mood and texture of the film serving to express the psychological effects of this state of mind rather than to dramatise causes. Each has reached a point of overt interior reflection, the high point of the relationship – the hotel bedroom scene – being the moment at which such reflections are most fully articulated and shared (although, again, the film does not exhibit the delaying of the narrative for the telling of stories about childhood, fantasies and dreams suggested by Bordwell as part of this dimension of art cinema narration).

What much of this adds up to, in Bordwell's version of art cinema and to some extent in *Lost in Translation*, is a mix of claims to 'objective' and 'subjective' forms of verisimilitude. A sense of objective realism is created through the general downplaying of narrative action and events, in favour of a focus on more quotidian aspects of life, a quality associated in the history of art cinema particularly with Italian post-war neorealism. *Lost in Translation* can be understood in this respect up to a point, even though its setting remains in some respects a heightened one. On the one hand, the whole point of the experiences undergone by

Bob and Charlotte is that they occur outside their daily routine, in the special context created by their removal to Tokyo (they also both enjoy a wealthy lifestyle at the hotel, a world that contrasts sharply with those often associated with 'grittier' forms of realism). It is this separation from the everyday that creates space for a critical reflection on the states of their lives. On the other hand, once this context is given, the actual experiences themselves are relatively quotidian and 'ordinary' in nature for the characters concerned, particularly when contrasted with the narrative material more typical of most mainstream/Hollywood features. The primary focus is on 'smaller' moments, observations and experiences, as suggested above, although this does not seem to aspire quite to the evocation of 'ordinary' or 'everyday' life examined in some instances of art cinema by Andrew Klevan.[10] In relation to Milos Forman's *Loves of a Blonde* (*Lásky jedné plavovláky*, 1965), for example, Klevan suggests, the characters 'engage with life in a half-hearted fashion, because they are not sure what they might be waiting for', a point that might also apply to the characterisation of Charlotte. 'The film holds back from defining clearly why the characters behave as they do', Klevan continues, 'and thus the narrative does not narrow itself down; it is not driven by a well-defined set of channelled objectives.'[11] A degree of such withholding might also be identified in *Lost in Translation*, but for the most part central character behaviour does seem quite clearly to be motivated by specific life experiences. The narrative here is not entirely narrowed down either, but is driven and channelled to a substantial extent by relatively familiar frameworks, most notably those which draw on the conventions of romantic comedy. The overall positioning of the film in this dimension is, once again, that of a hybrid status somewhere in between more and less narratively (or exceptional-circumstances-) driven alternatives.

There is also a subjective dimension to the narrative, however, located in the manner in which the experiences of the protagonists are presented to the viewer, particularly manifested in aspects of audio-visual style to be considered at greater length in the following sections of this chapter. In Bordwell's account, potentially incompatible elements of the objective and subjective are frequently reconciled in art cinema via the employment of ambiguity, a central dimension of many examples of the form. As much as anything, Bordwell suggests, art films 'ask to be puzzled over'.[12] This is not generally the case with *Lost in Translation* and is one of a number of ways in which the film goes considerably less far in demonstrating what have become recognised as conventional markers

Figure 13 Narrative withholding: Bob's unheard final whispered comments to Charlotte. © 2003 Universal Studios

of art cinema. Additional respects in which it does not really fit the bill include the absence of features identified by Bordwell such as narrative gaps or significant material that is not explained, disjunctions in temporal order such as less-than-clearly motivated flashbacks or the use of flash-forwards, and self-conscious narrative devices. *Lost in Translation* remains fully and clearly comprehensible at all times, even when the pace is at its most leisurely and in sequences that might not directly add anything to the linear development of plot.

The chief source of ambiguity in the film is the deliberately inaudible nature of Bob's comments to Charlotte during their farewell embrace. This is a notable feature of the film. The content of a key piece of dialogue – arguably *the* key piece, holding what would appear to be the single best indication of the likelihood of any future contact being maintained between the two, or any summary 'message' offered by the film – is denied to the viewer. Such a withholding of knowledge can be understood as a ploy of direct relevance to the wider positioning of the film, as suggested in the genre context in the previous chapter. A degree of openness is maintained which saves the film from having to commit itself entirely one way or the other, even if the realistic pros-pect of any continued contact seems rather faint. The overt nature of the device is such that it can also be taken to represent one instance of more self-conscious narrative material in *Lost in Translation*. This element of ambiguity is some considerable distance, however, from the more radical art-cinema practice, in some cases, of having major central ambiguities in the body of the text relating to elements such as uncertainty about the nature of a key event or events (as most famously manifested by Alain Resnais' *Last Year in Marienbad* [*L'année dernière à Marienbad*, 1961]) or the identity or fate of a significant character (the latter as in Michelangelo Antonioni's *L'avventura* [1960]). It does not impact on the principal fabric of the film, even if its influence is increased by its positioning at that privileged closing moment when any definitive 'answers' would be expected to be provided. The potential effect is similar in kind to one associated widely with art cinema – the explicit prompting of ongoing thought, speculation and/or discussion about the film – but it is a limited and contained version of such a phenomenon, offering a potentially pleasurable teasing of the viewer rather than any more radical aporia.

The low-key nature of the narrative of *Lost in Translation*, and the openness of the ending, are dimensions strongly appreciated by many of the Amazon respondents who report favourably on the film, but this is a dimension in which responses are highly polarised. A total of 1,027 of the 1,900 reviews comment on issues related to narrative, making it the most numerically prominent in the sample of all of the dimensions of the film analysed in this study (I have restricted this to comments that relate, explicitly or implicitly, to narrative form; to issues such as pace, structure, delineation of character and general narrative style and tenor, rather than those which relate to more substantive narrative content, even if the lines between the two are sometimes blurred and not so easy to distinguish). A total of 340 postings respond positively to the relative lack of narrative events (17.9 per cent of the entire sample or 33 per cent of those who comment on narrative), but these are outnumbered by the 551 who respond negatively (29 per cent of the total or 53.6 per cent of those who comment on narrative). Only fifty-nine of those who make reference to the low-key nature of the plotting do so in neutral terms, demonstrating the extent to which this is an issue that tends to divide viewers. Receptiveness to the narrative style of the film appears to be the most clear indicator of the extent to which respondents either do or do not fit the profile of what textual features establish as the ideal 'implied' viewer.

Many of the negative responses are very strongly put, more than half of these declaring the film to be 'boring' or sleep-inducing, a judgement made by 320 respondents (58 per cent of the negative responses, 16.8 per cent of the total sample or 31 per cent of those who comment on the narrative dimension; similar comments are also made by many of the negative respondents in the IMDb sample). Typical of these are the following, which are far from the most hyperbolic: 'The plot is slow, mediocre, predictable and boring' (Monica Graham, Weston, FL, 2 April 2006; 'this movie is so bad, so boring, so hopelessly bereft of plot, character, or any kind of story' (A. Fondacaro, Austin, TX, 30 December 2004). Declarations of boredom, or of struggling to stay awake through the film, also feature prominently among those who begin or headline their responses with comments related to narrative. Of 288 who give pride of place to this dimension, 238 (82.6 per cent) do so in negative terms, suggesting that the narrative qualities of *Lost in Translation* tend to loom most largely for those to whom they are a source of annoyance rather than pleasure. While some are deeply scathing, others are milder in their criticism. One declares the story to be 'a little dull for my tastes' (Jen Jen, New York, 16 April 2004) while another suggests that it is 'too subtle' and might have been better 'with a bit more melodrama to spice things up' (Dimitri-Yuriev, Houston, Texas, 19 February 2006). While much of the criticism of the narrative dimension is sweeping and absolute, other respondents seek to make it clear that they understand the point of the film, as in the following:

Actually folks I do get it. In fact I love thinking films and don't need extreme plot twists to keep me engaged. However, those who claim this is a wonderful character analysis are way off. I can't imagine weaker characters than these. (Simone Carpenter, New York, 5 July 2004)

Among those who respond positively to the low-key narrative approach, the most widespread judgement is that the film is 'subtle' in this dimension (although the term is also used more generally in other accounts in which it is not explicitly related to narrative or storytelling) and/or that it is character- rather than plot-driven. Some are more clearly positive than others. For one: 'It is a little slow, but it keeps your attention because you begin to love the characters' (Chad Abshier, San Diego, CA, 9 June 2005). A number of others respond to those who accuse the film of being boring by making the point that the film is at least partly *about* the experience of boredom, as part of its thematic dimension, for example: 'Many people call this film boring. Well, it is by no means supposed to be incredibly exciting . . . the movie is in part about tedium. It's just an aspect of isolation' (Z. Kaplan, Katy, Tx USA, 26 June 2005). For another, *Lost in Translation* 'is admittedly slow', but: 'There has never been a more honest or believable film ever. Because there is no conventional plot structure or character development, but instead pure experience and emotion' (R. A. McKenzie, New York, 3 August 2005). The impression created here, that the film is closer to reality, or unmediated experience, is a suggestion made in a number of the positive responses, although this is in some cases combined with an acknowledgement of aspects of more conventional structure. A good example of this mix is the following, which begins with a comment about the film being an expression of 'loneliness and isolation':

And it takes skill to pull this off – this movie could have quickly gone into non-narrative snoozeville. But although she [Coppola] follows the climax resolution format, the framework doesn't come poking through the story like it does in so many Hollywood films. It flows like a well documented life and that's high praise. (West End Girl, Austin, Texas, 21 January 2005)

As with some other aspects of the film, but to a greater extent, a substantial volume of the debate about the merits of its narrative style is related to the comments of other posters as well as to the text itself. A distinctly knock-about tone is adopted in some cases, and it is striking, when scrolling through some of the pages of reviews, to see such a strong polarity of opinion often being expressed from one posting to the next in relation to the same qualities of the film. Expressions of opinion about narrative often overlap with the kinds of distinction-marking, point-scoring comments considered in the previous chapter about the type of viewer for whom the film is designed. Many of the positive responses assert that a particular sensibility is required if this kind of narrative style is to be appreciated, a point also made by some who are more neutral in their own judgement. As one of the former puts it:

[the film] doesn't pander to hoary conventions or cheap passions, and its deliberate pacing and loose structure are actually products of the director's faith in the intelligence of her audience. She is counting on us to be both receptive and contemplative – sensitive enough to pick up on nuance and understatement without explicit narrative and broadcasted emotive cues. Based on the negative reviews on this site, it's too bad that her faith is misplaced in so many. (Barry C. Chow, Calgary, Alberta, Canada, 12 September 2004)

Visual style: 'subtlety' and 'nuance' as markers of distinction

A mixture of devices that might be associated with the objective and the subjective is also found in the visual texture of *Lost in Translation*, although the blend of the two and the effects that result are subtle and muted, in keeping with the general tenor of the film. The style of shooting, editing and lighting conforms, in most respects, to the tenets of the classical Hollywood continuity style. Distinctiveness is marked, in these formal dimensions, by relatively small touches, including expressive effects that contribute centrally to the atmospheric qualities of the film and the employment of devices that combine to signify its 'subtle', 'nuanced' or 'classy'/'prestige' status. Nothing is found, however, for which clear motivation is not available via matters of narrative and/or character, even if explanation for the employment of some devices might also exist at the level of the positioning of the film itself as to some extent distinct from the commercial mainstream.

One dynamic that can be identified fairly clearly in the shooting of *Lost in Translation* is a shift between sequences that are shot hand-held and relatively unsteadily and those shot with the camera locked-down on a tripod or moving more mechanically/smoothly via stable pan, track or dolly. These alternatives can be mapped not entirely but to a significant extent onto thematic dimensions of the film, particularly the major opposition established between the often lifeless and imprisoning nature of the world signified by the luxury hotel and the freedom and escape enjoyed by Bob and Charlotte in particular privileged moments associated with the development of their relationship. Many of the sequences shot in the hotel, including those which more clearly signify boredom, stultification or imprisonment, are shot in a stable, sometimes static manner. This includes a number of static 'deadpan' shots of Bob in the early stages of the film, for example: the shots of him towering over other occupants of the lift after his arrival; the flat, head-on shot of him sitting on his bed shortly afterwards. Another example is found later, during a sequence in which Bob speaks to his wife by telephone while lying in a luxurious bath. The sequence begins with an establishing long-shot taken from outside the immediate area of the bath, with Bob seen through an opening in the wall. A closer shot follows, as might be expected, as the conversation develops, but we are returned to the more distanced position for most of the remainder of the scene, for longer than would usually be expected,

Figure 14 Alienating hotel interiors: Bob shot from a distance in the bath. © 2003 Universal Studios

underlining the impression of strain and distance in the relationship. That this correlation of camera stasis and 'imprisoning' thematic dimensions is far from absolute is demonstrated, in one example, by the use of immobile, locked-down perspectives in the sequences involving Bob and Charlotte talking on his bed. This could be taken as signifying the 'serious and sober' aspect of their discussion of some of the more difficult realities of life and relationships – one overhead two-shot of the pair lying down is held for just over two minutes before a shift into a sequence of separate singles – but it is also much more positively coded than the other instances cited above.

Hand-held camerawork contributes to a number of overlapping effects, including the creation of an impression of verisimilitude in the evocation of certain aspects of the experiences of the protagonists (especially Charlotte) on the Tokyo streets and the underlining of the greater freedom experienced by the pair in the moments of escape that contribute to the cementing of their bond. A distinctly hand-held vérité impression is given to a number of sequences involving Charlotte's exploration of the city, although this is a subtle effect rather than the exaggeratedly unsteady aesthetic sometimes associated with hand-held footage elsewhere (in examples ranging from independent features such as *The Blair Witch Project* [1999] to studio productions including *Saving Private Ryan* [1998] or *The Bourne Supremacy* [2004]). When we see Charlotte on the subway train early in the film, for example, the camera is slightly unsteady rather than being jerked or shaken in a manner that draws overt attention to the device. As she moves to leave the carriage her image is obscured by the bodies of other passengers, another signifier of verité, of the action apparently being grabbed amid the contingencies of the 'real world' rather than every element being entirely staged; but this is brief and passing and, again, not drawn greatly to the attention of the viewer. The impression created here is of a certain kind of objectivity, an objective form of verisimilitude inhering in the distance created between character and camera. This is mixed with a more subjective impression in another sequence that follows a few scenes later involving the depiction of Charlotte on the bustling Tokyo streets.

In this case, the first shot is one that is soon marked as subjective, either a direct or approximate equivalent to the viewpoint of Charlotte. We are given a shot of a building at the Shibuya crossing, down much of the length of which plays a giant video screen showing the image of a dinosaur. The shot is at an upward angle with a number of umbrellas visible at the lower edge of the frame. Cut to an objectively situated shot of Charlotte among a crowd waiting at the roadside to cross, joining others in looking upwards (an eye-line that clearly implies a gaze at the video screen). This shot is almost wiped by the obstruction created by a passing vehicle, although it lingers fractionally afterwards. A medium-long shot is then provided of Charlotte walking left to right across the screen (and, by implication, the crossing, although it is out of view). The camera pans to follow her, continuing to do so across a cut back to a longer shot; at one point in the latter, part of the screen is obscured by another umbrella in the foreground. We are then returned to another view of the building with the video screen, which is now clearly located as a subjective image. The camera itself appears to be 'walking', with a slight bobbing motion, towards the building, a number of heads visible at the lower edge of the image. A cut follows to a long shot of Charlotte walking towards the camera, sometimes obscured by passing crowds, succeeded by a longer shot from another angle in which she continues to look upwards. We then return to the subjective shot, this time with no figures visible at the lower edge (presumably because we have moved closer to the building and the upward angle has increased). This shot then tilts downwards to look ahead at street level. Cut to medium close-up of Charlotte walking towards the camera and to screen-left (the same direction as in several previous shots). She walks closer to the camera and then disappears out of shot in the lower-left corner of the image (which suggests the use of a long lens taking the shot from a distance).

Figure 15 Subjective perspective: hand-held camera giving Charlotte's viewpoint on the streets (note umbrellas visible at lower edge of frame). © 2003 Universal Studios

Figure 16 Objective situation: the following shot establishes Charlotte's position and her upward gaze at the screen. © 2003 Universal Studios

This is a very conventional-seeming sequence in most if not all respects. A verité effect is created, as in the subway sequence, in the hand-held movement of the camera and the inclusion of elements that at times obstruct our view of the protagonist. This creates an impression that might be understood as one of 'freshness' and 'immediacy' and a slight 'edginess' – as compared with something entirely smooth, clear and seemingly precisely pre-planned down to every detail. But it also remains a carefully orchestrated sequence in its own way. Subjective and objective components might be expected to pull in opposite directions, but both are used here to create an overall impression of verisimilitude within which any such contradiction appears to be elided. This is at least partly because each element employs similar devices, including the partial obscuring of the image by passing detail in or at the margins of the frame: umbrellas, heads, moving vehicles. But it also fits a wider pattern found in many forms of commercial cinema that follow the model established by Hollywood continuity conventions: one in which more obviously distanced 'objective' shots from various positions are mixed with images taken from various degrees of proximity to the position of characters (the latter including what can be taken to be the equivalent of directly subjective shots of what characters see: eye-line-matching shots that usually follow shots of characters looking in a particular direction, even where no camera unsteadiness or the like is used more directly to mark the status of optical subjectivity). What ties the whole sequence clearly and legibly together is an entirely classical/conventional employment of standard continuity devices such as directional and eye-line matches. Another similar use of the slightly unsteady, hand-held camera is seen in a subsequent scene in which Charlotte wanders through a video-game arcade. The perspective shifts again between shots of the character and others clearly and conventionally marked as her view of the various game-screens and their players, together with some in which both Charlotte and gamers are in frame. Hand-held movement is evident in both types of shot, but again the unsteadiness is moderate, accompanied by occasional slight loss of focus.

Much the same kind of aesthetic is used in the sequences that follow Bob and Charlotte's first night out together, including a brief and slightly more overtly subjective shot of the former, the camera tilting down to his hand and forearm in the foreground as he receives his change at the bar of the club visited by the pair. A slightly more emphatic version of the mobile verité effect is employed during the scenes in which the couple and other members of their party are chased by the BB-gun wielding bartender, although it is still relatively modest in degree, especially given the heightened action involved in this instance. The hand-held quality is most obviously apparent as the two escape into a pachinko parlour. The camera follows their hurried movement down a narrow aisle and subsequently moves sideways along a series of rows, our view of Bob and Charlotte obscured as they pass the far end of each block. In the

Figure 17 Verité impression: 'wipe' effect created by hand-held camera move across aisles in the pachinko parlour. © 2003 Universal Studios

first case, the camera continues a single motion past the end of the aisle, which briefly obstructs the view. In the second, a cut is made during the 'wipe' effect created by the obstruction passing close to the lens, which adds to the slightly disjunctive effect (although it requires close re-viewing to establish the nature of the device). In the third and final instance, the wipe created when the camera is obscured by the aisle is blended into another wipe established by a passing vehicle in the shot that follows, taken from outside on the street. Here, a more obviously verité effect is created in a more distant perspective from the other side of the road to the point at which Bob and Charlotte emerge from the parlour, our view of the characters being obstructed by the movement of vehicles in the foreground. This is followed by a cut to a closer, quite unsteady hand-held shot, as Bob tries and fails to get a cab. We then return to the view from across the road, now given motivation other than arbitrary verité distance, as it becomes the viewpoint of a figure (a dark blur close to the camera) who calls them over to where another taxi awaits to reunite them with Charlotte's friends.

A distinctly hand-held impression remains to the fore in the following party/karaoke sequences that further develop the relationship between Bob and Charlotte. Camera movement remains modest but includes various slight shifts and readjustments and inexactitudes of framing (for example, in capturing Bob as he makes his first singing contribution and when he listens to Charlotte). As on some other occasions in the film, cuts are made into some quite brief moving shots, which create slight and passing impressions of disorientation. Focus is also lost in some moments, most clearly in one shot of Bob watching Charlotte's rendition of The Pretenders song, 'Brass in Pocket'. The shot structure seems more specifically motivated during Bob's second offering, a muted and 'heartfelt' performance of Roxy Music's 'More Than This', putting a clear emphasis on the developing relationship between the two principals. Part of the song is delivered with Bob, seated, in the foreground and to screen right. Charlotte is next to him, in the centre of the frame, with her Japanese friend 'Charlie Brown' (Fumihiro Hayashi) to the left. At first, Bob is in focus, the images of Charlotte and Charlie blurred. The focus then shifts to Charlotte, leaving Bob blurred, as she looks at him and then away, in a manner that suggests that she is slightly embarrassed but also touched by his rendition. We then return to a shot that began the sequence, framing his head and shoulders as he sings directly to her (the pink wig that Charlotte is now wearing being visible as a blurry unfocused mass at screen left). A cut is made to an answering single shot of Charlotte looking at him, followed by a return to the previous shot of Bob, as he brings the song and sequence to an end. What happens here, very clearly, is that the more general rendition of the karaoke experience becomes subordinated to the task of underlining the current nature and development of the relationship between the two. Each is isolated, along with their emotional state, first by the shift of focus and then by the separate shots in which they are extracted from the wider scene. This is another entirely conventional usage, both in the specific devices employed and the broader process of which they are a part.

The hand-held camerawork used in these sequences does appear to have some direct relationship with the moments of greater freedom experienced by the central characters, both separately and, more significantly, when shared. The same goes for its employment during their second night out when they escape from the sex-dancing bar. Their dash outside is rendered in one of the most unsteady shots in the film, a downward-looking slightly high-angle shot that moves in wavering style through the crowd on the street. The camera follows them as they run out into the road; a cut is made into another mobile shot from the other side of the characters, and then to another position from behind in which the camera swings around with them before they are brought to a halt by the sight of a passing truck that carries a huge image of Bob's whisky advertisement on its side. Hand-held mobility contributes significantly here to the impression of exhilarating freedom and escape enjoyed by the protagonists, as it does somewhat less strikingly in the earlier incident involving the BB gun. In the more general scenes of Charlotte on the streets, what is implied might be a broader spirit of freedom and exploration, albeit one that is mixed with an element of disorientation. In the partying and karaoke sequences, the shooting and editing style can be seen to contribute importantly, if only implicitly, to the creation of the impression of relaxed informality that creates space for the relationship between Bob and Charlotte to develop beyond the more restricted confines of their earlier meetings in the hotel. In each of these cases, whether the impressions appear objective or subjective, the aesthetic is directly related to the location shooting strategy outlined in Chapter 1, the lightweight and flexible 'guerrilla style' that combines the practical limitations of low-budget production with the creation of expressive effects well suited to the material (the same goes for the similar exigencies, and expressive effects, involved in the shooting of improvised performances such as those given during the karaoke sequences).

At all of its stages, the central relationship is developed cinematically through the use of very conventional/classical devices, including some of the early parallels created through editing suggested in the previous chapter. The first clear connection between Bob and Charlotte, when sitting separately in the bar, is indicated through conventional matching of eye-lines and directions of looks, as they share wry smiles after the performance of the lounge band. A more elaborate orchestration is employed in the second bar contact, the one in which Charlotte is bored by the company of Kelly and one of the members of the band that John is photographing. The sequence includes a shot looking over Bob's shoulder (he is very out of focus and blurred) across the room to focus on Charlotte's table, reinforcing the impression already created in the scene that he is looking in her direction. The same viewpoint is maintained subsequently as she walks towards him and it becomes one pole in an exchange of shot/reverse-shots (as he jokes about the prison break). A final closer shot of her marks not just greater physical proximity but also suggests the achievement of another stage in the development of their relationship. Further sequences in the bar are constructed through assemblages mostly of two-shots and shot/reverse-shots of each character. In their first substantial exchange of dialogue and life experiences, a sizeable gap is left between the two when framed from across a counter in two-shot, sitting next to each other (accompanied by cuts away to respective over-the-shoulder shots/reverse-shots of each). In their final encounter in the bar, they are closer and facing directly towards each other (a sequence again broken up by the use of closer-up shot/reverse-shot pairs), making more sustained and deeper contact, as would be expected at this stage in the relationship. The lighting on each occasion creates a heightened and romantic impression – again, entirely according to dominant convention – a golden light being cast on their faces and Charlotte's blonde hair, against dark backgrounds.

In these and numerous other instances, Coppola favours shallow planes of focus, created through the use of long lenses, to highlight particular elements within the frame. These are used on some occasions to separate Bob and Charlotte from the background, a visual reinforcement of the broader basis of their relationship as defined partly through distinction from the worlds by which they are surrounded (this is in keeping with a broader tradition in which flatness of space has been used to signify the trapped status of characters[13]). This is an approach that also seems to connote a certain 'classy' style of imagery on the part of the director and the cinematographer Lance Acord. First coming into widespread use in the 1960s, according to David Bordwell, the defocused planes created by the long lens 'helped associate the look with lyrical romance.'[14] The use of shallow focus in *Lost in Translation*, or in some cases the shifting of focus within a single frame, gives the impression of careful design and control of the image. It is a relatively overt formal choice, creating noticeable areas of blurriness, although it has the merit for this region of the cultural landscape of also appearing modest in its claims to attention, as opposed to the use of devices that might signify a less nuanced form of 'flashiness' or 'showiness', an issue to which we return below.

Blurry image quality plays a distinctive role in the overall aesthetic of *Lost in Translation*, beyond its use as indistinct background to narrative/character events. It has an expressive quality in its own right. In the first and last of the two bar encounters cited above, the gap between the principals (greater or lesser) is filled with the blurry images of aircraft warning lights on the buildings opposite the hotel: pulsating red blobs that add extra visual interest to the screen, softened by their out-of-focus status. Whether they should be taken to signify anything more specific might remain subject to debate. If nothing else, they can be taken as another reminder of the flashing-neon/light quality that figures consistently throughout the film as one of the signifiers of 'Tokyo-ness', although here given a muted quality that seems less strident and less associated

Figure 18 Expressive blur: near-abstract patters created by lights reflected over Charlotte's face on taxi window glass. © 2003 Universal Studios

with disorientation than is the case in some other instances. 'Red light' could also be taken to imply something more sexual, actual or potential, in the relationship between the two, although such an implication might be judged to be more 'crude' and 'obvious' than the kinds of qualities with which the film more generally seems to want to associate itself. It also happens that the most prominent lights in each scene form a line that coincides quite closely with the eye-line established between the two characters, although that might again seem rather too crude a device (almost a join-the-dots from one to the other) to have been the outcome of deliberate design (see cover image).

Blurring is also used to more clearly motivated effect in some sequences, in addition to moments that signify briefly the verité nature of some hand-held footage. When Bob and Charlotte are being driven back to the hotel after their first night out, hand-held shots from inside the car (of the passing cityscape, a bridge and the road) include one moment when a shot looking forward down the street goes very out of focus, reducing the vehicles ahead to mere blobs of light – signifying, it seems, the nodding-off to sleep of one or both of the characters, as does an earlier moment when a jump-cut occurs between two similar but slightly different shots of the road ahead (it transpires that Bob is asleep in the car, Charlotte looking out the window). This sequence continues with shots of passing neon and a reverse-angle of Charlotte's face overlaid with blurring neon reflections in the window glass. Another, closer shot of passing buildings/lights is followed by a closer shot of Charlotte behind the glass, the blurry lights forming more abstract patterns across her face. A couple of shots later we are given a view of very blurred and unfocused passing lights as if seen from her perspective, again verging on the abstract. This can be taken either as part of the broader evocation of the city neon offered by the film, part of the 'hypnotic' quality of the cityscape, or as suggesting another lapse into sleep (when we catch up with the couple back at the hotel, it is Bob who is carrying a sleeping Charlotte).

There are some other moments when blurred images come close to the abstract in *Lost in Translation*. One is an image of Charlotte standing in front of her hotel window in which the focus is on the distant buildings opposite and her figure is considerably distorted by the degree of blur (her neck seems to be rendered unnaturally thin). Typically, though, this shot is held only very briefly, before John enters the room behind her, comes into shot, embraces her and the focus shifts onto the couple, who end up in a sharp near-silhouette composition in front of the window. That blurry lights and/or shifting planes of shallow focus might serve as a signifier of a certain kind of cultural status is suggested more explicitly by their similar deployment in the brand image constituted by the Focus Features logo that appears at the start of the film and other Focus releases. A highly blurred pattern of colours shifts slightly as it moves into greater focus, forming a overlapping series of circles, still quite hazy and abstract rather than sharp, on top of which appears the name of the distributor in clear focus, all but the 'o' of 'Focus', which remains fuzzy in echo of the background; a logo that could have been created with *Lost in Translation* specifically in mind. The logo was designed, clearly, to express the name of the distributor but the particular image effect that results might also be taken to signify a specific kind of cinematic quality.

Shots of the cityscape form an important part of the visual fabric of the film, in most cases not abstracted but doing more than routine duty in the establishment of location. These include both the neon signage so strongly associated with modern Tokyo and wider vistas as seen from the windows of the hotel. From the start, Tokyo is first evoked in neon form, in the sequence of shots intercut with Bob's drive from the airport. The final one of these seems to perform a more expressive function than the others, a closer shot filled with the image of one neon sign that pulsates in a hypnotic pattern (suggesting, perhaps, Bob's state of jet-lagged disorientation). Blurry lights also form the background to an early scene featuring Charlotte's insomnia in her hotel room. Cityscapes are used at

Figure 19 Cityscape: the start of the lengthy pan across Charlotte in the hotel window. © 2003 Universal Studios

Figure 20 Charlotte framed in 'vulnerable' posture as the camera moves behind her. © 2003 Universal Studios

Figure 21 The camera continues, implacably, turning away from and past the character. © 2003 Universal Studios

times in conventional establishing-shot style as punctuating devices, or
markers of temporal shifts (for example, an evening view that precedes
Bob's return to the hotel after his first shoot). But more extended vistas
are also supplied, particularly in association with Charlotte's isolation
and unhappiness in the hotel. Her characteristic position is seated in
or close to the picture windows of her room, framed against the back-
drop of the city, images that suggest her smallness and vulnerability in
comparison with the vast scale of the 'alien' urban environment. The
most notable example is an extended pan that comes at Charlotte's
most isolated moment, immediately after the departure of John for his
out-of-town photo shoot. The camera starts with a movement to the left
across the view out of the window before coming alongside and behind
Charlotte, who sits looking out with her arms wrapped around bare
knees, itself a pose that suggests smallness and vulnerability. The pan
continues, hand-held, around her so that we can see her face, and then
keeps on going, turning away from Charlotte as it moves around and the
city itself again fills the frame. We then cut to another pan returning in
the other direction, although starting at a point closer to Charlotte than
that at which the previous pan ended, turning back around to end behind
her. It is notable that the first movement of the pan does not stop when
it reaches the view of Charlotte's face, as might most conventionally be
expected. In that case, the pan might still be sufficiently extended, and
offering so striking an image of the city, to have performed more than
merely an establishing function. Continuing the camera movement not
just past the character but also emphasising this with the turn away
from her in the latter stages seems to strengthen quite considerably the
more expressive qualities of the shot (the fact that it seems to be saying
something about her emotional state of isolation or withdrawal at that
moment in the diegesis), as does the addition of the shorter pan back in
the opposite direction (although the latter does also re-focus the sequence
on the character, itself a more conventional quality).

Shots such as the lengthy pan across the cityscape and Charlotte in the
window contribute to the generally unhurried pace of *Lost in Translation*,
one of the most striking features of the film, as suggested above at the
level of narrative. The standard measure of pace in visual terms is
average shot length (ASL), calculated by dividing the running time by
the total number of individual shots. *Lost in Translation*'s ASL comes out
at 6.5 seconds, a figure that locates it at the top end of the Hollywood
norm for its time, an average range for all genres of three to six seconds

at the turn of the century, according to David Bordwell.[15] While the fastest-cut films of the period, usually action movies (including, perhaps, the imaginary example in which Kelly appears), have an ASL as low as two seconds, the figure for *Lost in Translation* is another indicator that falls in the region that might be expected for an indie/Indiewood film of this kind: higher than most Hollywood films but not as high as that found in indie films that lean further towards the domain of art cinema in style.[16] ASL can be, as Bordwell suggests, 'the major distinguishing mark of off-Hollywood directors', other examples including the films of Jim Jarmusch, Hal Hartley and Whit Stillman.[17] An ASL of 6.5 seconds marks *Lost in Translation* as standing against a trend in recent decades towards ever-increasing rates of cutting, a tendency that, as Bordwell suggests, spreads far wider than action cinema to include genres such as romantic comedy with which the film has some elements in common (and that includes the construction of dialogue-based scenes as well as the mounting of action set-pieces). As in many other respects, however, Coppola departs only relatively from the mainstream norm, the use of longer-held and/or more static shots being balanced by some quicker editing and the employment in certain instances of devices such as cutting into moving shots that are also associated by Bordwell with the 'intensified continuity' characteristic of the contemporary Hollywood mainstream. Some of the hand-held sequences examined above also contribute to a 'busyness' and slight 'edginess' of visual imagery that also seems more in keeping with mainstream trends.

All of the visual qualities detailed in this chapter have clear motivation at the level of matters relating to character experience, relationships and narrative, as suggested above and as would also be expected of a feature produced, distributed and exhibited in the relatively mainstream arenas of the indie or Indiewood sectors. Devices that, in other usage, might imply allegiance to more radical types of cinema are effectively 'contained' in this manner, serving expressive purposes rather than offering more challenging or disorienting experiences to the viewer. One additional example that underlines this point is the use of a series of jump-cuts in a sequence that features Charlotte in her room after she and Bob return to the hotel on their second night out on the town and before the two get together for their heartfelt discussion on his bed. The sequence begins with a tilt downwards from the window to Charlotte lying in bed. A cut is then made abruptly forwards, marking an unspecified lapse of time, into an already-started action, in which she is sitting up in bed and pulling on a vest. She then leans back and a jump-cut is made to a slightly closer shot of Charlotte leaning forward. Another jump-cut gives us Charlotte leaning away from the camera and over the far side of the bed, then sitting up and resting her arms on her knees. Another takes us to her sitting on the side of the bed, pulling on a cardigan. The next shot, for which the continuity seems slightly more established, has Charlotte's image reflected in the window as she walks across the room. We then cut to a shot in which she is now sitting in a chair and picks up a magazine. Then cut to a higher angle of Charlotte on the chair, apparently deep in thought and without the magazine. The next shot depicts a note being slid under her door. Entirely clear continuity comes in the following shot, Charlotte's reaction to seeing the appearance of the note, after which she stands and walks across the room (the latter seen in window reflection). We then see her walk up to the door, pick up the note and read it, in subsequent shots that abide by continuity norms.

What happens in the first part of this sequence, up to the appearance of the note, is that gaps are left in what would usually be expected of a series of shots assembled according to the dominant conventions of continuity editing. Charlotte's position shifts abruptly on several occasions and we are deprived of a clear shot-by-shot impression of exactly what happens between one moment and the next, or how much time has passed in the intervals that are skipped. This is slightly disorienting, although far from radically so. For one thing, it is clear that the jumps are relatively small and it is easy for the viewer to fill in the gaps. Viewers have probably also become relatively familiar with the use of jump-cuts in this manner, far more so than when they were employed to notable effect in examples of art cinema such as the early films of Jean-Luc Godard, especially *Breathless* (*À bout de souffle*, 1960). Such devices have been employed as small touches, rather than as radical departures, by numerous filmmakers in the intervening decades. And as in many such uses, the employment of jump-cuts here by Coppola and her editor is clearly motivated by character experience, rather than having a seemingly arbitrary (and therefore potentially more disorienting) effect. The awkward, jumpy quality of the sequence provides an expression of Charlotte's restlessness (it is akin, in this respect, to the opening sequence of *Bonnie and Clyde* [1967], a key product of the Hollywood 'Renaissance' of the later 1960s to mid-1970s and a film directly influenced by French *nouvelle vague* filmmakers such as Godard). It can be understood as an expression of her continuing insomnia, generally, but also more specifically in this sequence in terms of unresolved issues or tensions in her relationship with Bob; or, unresolved tensions about the nature of the relationship for the *viewer* that are addressed to a large extent in the sequence into which it leads. However exactly it is interpreted, the crucial fact when it comes to placing the film in the wider spectrum is that the device appears to be motivated and to serve a clear narrative/character-related purpose.

For most viewers, the kinds of visual qualities examined above are unlikely to be identified as such, as is suggested by the Amazon responses examined below. They are more likely to function on a subliminal level in the creation of particular impressions, another indicator of the extent to which they are integrated into the broadly mainstream end of serving or reinforcing conventional dramatic ends. Here, again, what counts in the marking of relative positions in the cinematic spectrum is the *degree* of departure from the norm found in any particular example. If the pan across the cityscape as seen from the window in which Charlotte sits is taken to mark some departure from the norm, in its relative temporal extension and its initial continuation past the position of the protagonist, it might be compared with the use of a more conventional panning estab-lishing shot, in one direction, but also with more radical equivalents in the other. The latter would include greatly extended shots employed by Jon Jost, an independent filmmaker whose work has resolutely refused the kinds of compromises required for the achievement of commercial distribution. Jost's films combine relatively conventional feature narra-tive elements (such as character relationships and conflicts) with lengthy sequences that appear to serve little such immediate purpose and that are as a result likely to draw the viewer's attention to the formal dimension itself. These include a series of pans around the space of a café in *The Bed You Sleep In* (1993) that extends without event for some five minutes, well in excess of anything that would be expected in the classical style.[18] Similar points can be made about some of the other relatively more distinctive or expressive devices employed by Coppola. If highly out-of-focus images are included on occasion, other than in the background, it is as important to note their brief, passing nature as it is to draw them to attention as markers of difference. To have used such images more substantially, unless clearly motivated by some altered state of character consciousness, would be to shift, again, towards the territory of a more resolutely indie or art cinema, as for example in some sequences in a film such as Harmony Korine's *Julien Donkey-Boy* (1999).[19]

Much of the more distinctive visual texture of *Lost in Translation* is dedicated to the creation of mood and atmospherics, particularly in the evocation of aspects of the Tokyo landscape and its impact on the principal characters, as is suggested in much of the detail considered above. Visual style and narrative structure work here to much the same end, a significant part of each being dedicated to the provision of time and space to dwell on material that might normally be expected to be relegated rather more to the background than is the case in this instance. If this is true in narrative terms of the sequence in which we see Charlotte travel to Kyoto, for example, much the same could be said of the imagery that results. More time than necessary to establish the bare fact that she is travelling by train is given, at the start, to the shots from the windows, as Charlotte contemplates the passing landscape. A similarly leisurely approach, marked cinematically as 'atmospheric', is given to Charlotte's wanderings after her arrival, beginning with what appears to be a subjectively oriented moving upward-angle shot catching the sun shining through the leaves of the trees overhead, the light creating the 'arty' impression of lens flare in the image. A generally unhurried impression is created by the entire Kyoto sequence, in which the film seems to be going at the pace of the character's thoughts, seemingly without any particular direction other than marking out a need for time and space for reflection (although her witnessing of a traditional wedding procession has some thematic resonance, considered in the following chapter). This is certainly one respect in which the formal dimensions of *Lost in Translation* have something in common with those of *The Virgin Suicides* in a manner that could be taken as an indication of the auteur presence in Coppola's first two features, as suggested in the previous chapter.

If certain markers of formal distinction are present in *Lost in Translation*, whether or not identified with those of Coppola's debut feature, it is worth asking towards whom exactly such markers might be targeted (implicitly, at least, even if this is not assumed to be a conscious process of distinction-marking on the part of the individual filmmaker). If their presence and effect might remain implicit for most viewers, particular constituencies can be identified for which they might be of more overt appeal. These might include academic commentators such as myself and other 'serious' followers of this part of the American film landscape. More importantly, though, as far as the fate of such a work is concerned, such dimensions might be of appeal to critics at the more serious/substantial end of the reviewing spectrum, and might thus loom more largely in the general placing and evaluation of the film than would otherwise be the case. That said, it is noticeable that mainstream critics tend to use rather vague and impressionistic phrases to account for the visual qualities of the film, rather than detailing the use of particular devices, while some ignore this dimension altogether in favour of their focus on elements such as plot/character and performance. The latter is the case for the broader market *New York Post* and *USA Today*, which might not be surprising, but also for some more substantial publications. *The New York Times*, generally considered to carry the greatest single agenda-setting weight of any print review source, restricts itself to very broad references to style and mood: *Lost in Translation* offers 'stylized lonesomeness' and risks being 'dismissed as self-consciously moody rather than registering as a mood piece'.[20] The *Los Angles Times*, another publication considered to be among the more influential, offers no specific reference to visuals or style at all. Neither does Roger Ebert in the Chicago *Sun-Times*.

The *Boston Globe* is typical of the kinds of references that tend to be made where they are found, in its description of the film as 'lovely, lapidary', its comment that it is 'longer on atmosphere and observation than story, but you don't mind' and its reference to Coppola's knack for 'casually framing a shot that you'd want to hang on your wall.'[21] The *San Francisco Chronicle* is similar in its descriptive phrases ('gorgeous', 'delicate, beautifully observed') and its inclusion of 'the magical framing of Tokyo's neon canyons' in a list of qualities admired by the critic, as is the *Seattle Post-Intelligencer* in its references to 'a beautifully composed atmosphere of isolation' and the comment in relation to Coppola that 'Her eye for Tokyo is inspired'.[22] One of the more sustained attempts to capture an impression of the formal qualities of the film is made by Stephanie Zacharek in Salon.com, although her more specific comments are directed at the level of narrative:

Instead of unfolding in precise pleats, [Coppola's] movies unfurl like bolts of silk. There are no handy place markers between scenes to help us tick off how many minutes are likely to have passed between this or that point of conflict and the denouement.[23]

On the visuals, with a credit for the cinematographer, Zacharek relies on the same kind of generality ('it was shot, beautifully, by relative newcomer Lance Acord]') as those cited above.

In none of these cases, or numerous others in major US newspapers and magazines, is any specific detail given of particular visual devices that constitute or contribute to the effects described. Instead, it seems, specific formal qualities of the kind analysed in this chapter provide the grounds for translation by critics into more generic (and in this case, usually posi- tive) terms such as beauty, stylishness and subtlety, the general tenor of which is relatively similar across the board. None of this is surprising, given the more generally evaluative remit of press reviews and the fact that they are usually based on attendance at one preview screening rather than the opportunity for close analysis of individual sequences. Some critics might be more capable than others of identifying more exactly the sources of the qualities they praise in general terms, but part of the process of critical mediation can be understood to be one in which the detailed and specific – dependent on more expert knowledge – is con- verted into the general and accessible, and oriented more towards evalu- ation than to analysis. The general impressions conveyed in this manner are likely to contribute just as much to the 'placing' of the film in the wider spectrum. Key terms such as 'subtle' and 'understated', whether used broadly or in relation to specific dimensions of a film, have a par- ticular currency as markers of distinction in the indie and Indiewood sectors, alongside more generally valued descriptors such as 'gorgeous' or 'stylish'. Terms such as 'subtle' or 'nuanced', which I have used myself less reflexively at times in the preceding pages, certainly appear to embrace the kinds of qualities for which Coppola strove, as indicated on several occasions above. The overall impression that seems to have been sought is one in which markers of distinction are provided but do not wish to advertise their presence too loudly. Hence the 'nuanced' use of verité effects such as relatively minor degrees of instability or obstruction of the camera and reliance on shallow focus or 'subtle' lighting effects for the creation of a 'classy' image quality: effects not designed to be over- emphatic or 'obvious' in character, but to appeal to a notion of the 'dis- cerning' viewer with a more finely tuned level of appreciation. This can be set in contrast to the more heightened versions of intensified continu- ity (extremely fast cutting, outlandish camera movements, etc.) described by Bordwell as offering 'an audacious style that parades virtuosity' in a manner that might be considered to be 'crude' or 'obvious'.[24]

The difference between what is understood or constructed as the 'subtle' and the 'obvious' can be understood through Pierre Bourdieu's notion of the distinctions made by particular social groups in the con- sumption of a whole range of consumer products, especially those related to arts and culture.[25] Bourdieu draws a broad contrast between the typical taste preferences of the upper, middle and lower classes. Inhabitants of the lower classes, according to this account, tend to favour products that offer what are understood to be more immediate pleasures in which form is subordinate to function. An example of this kind of orientation is provided in a study of audiences of the mainstream action film *Judge Dredd* (1995) by Martin Barker and Kate Brooks. For some viewers, oriented specifically towards the pleasures of the action-adventure genre, the overwhelming emphasis of their responses is on the experience of the thrills offered by the film in the present tense. What the film has to offer is, exactly, 'obvious, it's all there on-screen' and a marker of distinction in this case is 'to separate yourself from the "analysts"', from those who might probe such a film for any other significance.[26] At the opposite end of the spectrum, for Bourdieu, is an aesthetically oriented disposition, located in class fractions high in cultural capital (particularly intellectuals and artists), in which the emphasis is put on form rather than function.

If we try to situate the qualities offered by *Lost in Translation* into this kind of scheme, they would occupy a position somewhere in the middle ground: not immediately obvious but equally far from being oriented towards an appreciation of form for its own sake. The nuanced forms employed by the film serve quite clear functions, as indicated above, but functions that might not be immediately transparent or that do not offer instant pay-off or gratification of the kind associated with some of the intensified devices used in contemporary action cinema. Relatively small differences in form serve relatively different functions, rather than being taken to a point at which form is likely to become the issue in itself. This can be said of the aspects of both narrative and visual style considered in this chapter. To appreciate and take pleasure from such qualities, a certain level of cultural capital is required, but not the specialist resources required for the enjoyable consumption of 'higher' art forms such as those found towards the avant-garde or experimental end of the scale. The viewer of *Lost in Translation* is not asked to work particularly hard to fathom the nature, purpose or meaning of the film, and does not require any high level of expertise in order to do so in general terms. But the film does offer reward to those who, as a result of their social upbringing and education, have learned to appreciate and invest in notions such as subtlety and nuance in the deployment of what remain broadly mainstream and accessible forms (how this kind of positioning might relate to particular social classes or other groups, along with some qualifications relating to the use of schemas such as that suggested by Bourdieu, I have considered at greater length elsewhere[27]).[28]

The finer details of visual and other formal qualities might also be appreciated by another small minority audience, but one that can also be of importance to the individual filmmaker: the audience comprised by others in the business and related arts. A similar point is made by David Bordwell in the somewhat different context of what he sees as an *excess* of narrative unification or extravagance in some contemporary studio features.[29] If audiences and critics play the most obviously important roles in the evaluation and recognition of filmmakers, the opinions of other filmmakers can also be of significance, both for the individuals themselves and for the development of their wider reputation. Impressing their most immediate confederates is unlikely to be the sole or primary motivation for the use of particular formal nuances or subtleties of the kind found in *Lost in Translation*, as might be the case in the more rarefied territory of the avant-garde or the experimental (the latter existing in regions of cultural production defined by Bourdieu as operating according to the 'autonomous principle', in which works are produced primarily for an audience of fellow producers in a realm that lies outside the laws of the marketplace and in which all that counts is artistic prestige[30]). The demands of the more immediate commercial market are too pressing for that to be the case, for any feature production that seeks relatively mainstream distribution, but it can be a secondary motivation of not inconsiderable significance. This might be particularly the case for a second-time feature director such as Coppola, for whom *Lost in Translation* was an opportunity to prove the critical success of *The Virgin Suicides* not to have been a fluke and to demonstrate her auteur credentials in a work based on her own material rather than one of adaptation (and for a filmmaker who occupies a world such as that of Coppola, coming from a background including the heavy overshadowing presence of her father and surrounded by a distinctive creative community including those of her own generation within which she might be expected to want to make her mark).

Viewer responses as measured by the Amazon sample used in this book are similar in some respects to those of professional critics, tending towards the use of shorthand phrases such as 'beautiful images' and 'stunning cinematography' or terms that highlight the 'atmospheric' or 'poetic' effects created by the visual style of the film. Visual style is cited by far fewer respondents than narrative, a total of 355 out of the 1,900 (18.6 per cent), which might be explained by the fact that its narrative distinctiveness is a more prominent feature of the film (it might also be a dimension that most such respondents find easier to comment upon in more concrete terms). Among these, however, a far higher level of agreement is found. A large majority both praises this dimension of the film (303, 15.9 per cent of the total sample or a striking 85 per cent of those who comment on the visuals) and does so in the kinds of brief or passing phrases cited above (281, 14.8 per cent of the total or 79 per cent of those who comment on this dimension). The number of negative responses is small, just twenty-four (1.2 per cent of the total or 6.7 per cent of those who comment on the visuals), while eighteen offer mixed responses. It is also notable that a number of those who approve of the visuals do so while making negative judgement of the film as a whole, qualities relating to cinematography or other aspects of the visual style being seen in some cases as some compensation – but often insufficient – for what are identified as other or more general shortcomings. Examples of this tendency include one who headlines their response: 'Nice photography, that's about it' (Blue Eyes, nyc, 20 June 2005) and another who comments that the film is 'boring, but very beautiful' (derrotista, Cadiz, Spain, 1 March 2005).

Terms of praise used for the visuals are in most cases undeveloped, as might be expected from viewers generally likely to be unschooled in the vocabulary required for closer and more specific analysis. Typical phrases include the following: 'the visual texture is outstanding' (P. Freeman, Austin, TX, 13 September 2005), 'vivid and often surrealistic imagery' (Ross Pezl, Chicago, 30 April 2007) and 'beautiful and sometimes haunting images' (Roidefromage, Denver, CO, 9 July 2008). In none of these cases is any attempt made to unpack what might more exactly be meant by such terms. Some struggle, with mixed degrees of success, to express what they mean in a little more detail while one is happy to concede that: 'I have no technical or artistic explanation for why I loved this film. I just know that as a whole it completely mesmerized me and left me feeling somehow lucky to have seen it' (Mark Waddell, Anchorage, Ak. United States, 28 May 2004). Only nine respondents make comments that go into very specific detail in their praise. Two refer to the use of shallow planes of focus considered above. One of these gives credit to cinematographer Acord, 'who uses low depth of field to isolate the characters and still keep Tokyo glittering in the background' (A Customer, 18 March 2004) while another refers to how Coppola

will, from time to time, let images slide in and out of focus and/or have the centre of the frame far from the action, catching bits of each event but never really focusing the scene on any one character. (Rob 'Revuman', New York, NY USA, 18 February 2004)

Another two make reference to the use of lights reflected on car windows, described by one as 'a stunning technique that Coppola utilizes more than once in the film' (PM Elam, 21 March 2005) and cited by another in the context of references to the literary Symbolist movement (A Customer, 22 February 2004). Acord's cinematography is 'beautiful' for one respondent, 'barely augmenting natural light most of the time so it doesn't get that "Hollywood" look' (A Customer, 21 March 2004), while several others praise the film in terms of what one describes as its 'realistic, almost documentary-like style' (FairiesWearBoots8272, USA, 10 February 2004). Those who dig down at all into any specifics remain a small minority, however, particular aesthetic practices tending to be translated into more hazy and impressionistic terms for the majority of those who comment on this dimension of the film.

Entirely negative responses to the visual style of *Lost in Translation* are also few in number, although one or two dismiss the cinematography in terms such as 'horrible' (A Customer, 15 April 2004). The manner in which the visuals are criticised by some implies that these are framed as counterweights to the volume of praise given by others, as suggested by two comments made in relatively later postings: 'there is no beautiful cinematography or any interesting camera works [*sic*]' (Richard Se, Singapore, 14 January 2005); 'not "visually stunning" or "revolutionary" or even plain "good"' (T. D. Ferguson, Atlanta, GA USA, 29 October 2004). Some complain that what others describe as 'beautiful cinematography' is little more than 'travelogue', referring to the Tokyo cityscapes, which are objects of praise for many, while several object to either the hand-held camerawork or the instances of jumpy editing (or a combination of both). On balance, however, analysis of the Amazon sample suggests that, where they provide a source of comment, the visual qualities of the film are viewed as one of its least controversially positive dimensions, a trend that also applies to its use of music and other sound effects.

Music: the centrality of atmospherics, texture and mood

If specific visual and narrative qualities are central to the particular impressions created by *Lost in Translation*, in terms of both the manner in which the diegetic world is evoked and the broader positioning of the film as 'subtle' and 'nuanced', it is not possible to give anything like a full account of these without considering the use of music, a key contribution to the texture of the piece. It is very often the music that does the primary work in overtly establishing tone and mood, having shaped the evolution of the project from an early stage as a result of the mixes put together for Coppola by Brian Reitzell during the writing process, elements of which (including tracks by Squarepusher, Death in Vegas and the Jesus and Mary Chain) found their way into the final product; the music was also taken to Japan during location scouting ahead of shooting.[31] The role played by the music is another respect in which the film departs from classical/mainstream norms only to a limited extent. For music to function in this manner is far from uncommon, as can be demonstrated by an examination of almost any Hollywood feature. If it figures to a larger extent that usual in *Lost in Translation*, the reason is that qualities such as 'mood' and 'atmospherics' (sometimes rather vaguely defined) themselves play a greater than normal part in the constitution of the substance of the film, as has already been suggested in a number of contexts above. Music plays a major role in evoking the dreamy, narcotised, semi-detached impressions of jet-lag that feature in several sequences in the film, both literally and as an emblem of a more general experience of distance, alienation and/or disorientation. It figures in some ways more obviously and recognisably in performing this function than the visuals to which it is more than just accompaniment, making what is probably the largest single contribution to the widespread understanding of the film as a 'mood piece' as much as a production based around linear narrative progression. The music itself is also chiefly of an 'indie' variety, bringing a specific cultural cachet of its own that contributes to the broader placing of the film as a whole.[32] The use of music to evoke character experience itself remains entirely within classical norms, the markers of difference here as elsewhere often being those of degree rather than kind. Music also serves some more immediately conventional purposes in which it can be understood to constitute part of the narrative infrastructure, in ways that might to greater or lesser degrees be associated with the 'subtle/nuanced' characteristics examined in the previous section.

From the early sequence in which Bob awakes on his way into the city from the airport, the music plays a role equal to if not dominating that of the visuals in the evocation of his jet-lagged state. The alternating images of Bob and the passing neon streets are played to the accompaniment of

'Girls' by Death in Vegas, hushed breathy non-verbalised vocals with a simple guitar accompaniment creating a drifting, ethereal and somewhat dreamy quality that precisely captures the impressions of temporal and spatial disjunction characteristic of jet-lagged arrival in distantly foreign climes. A similarly bleary, half-asleep quality is conveyed by the use of 'Sometimes' by My Bloody Valentine to complement the hand-held camerawork, jump-cuts and blurry visuals employed in the staging of Bob and Charlotte's taxi ride back to the hotel after their first night out together: the characteristically thickly textured guitar work of Kevin Shields in the foreground, over a quieter, more lyrical voice and other instrumentation. The distinctive sound associated with Shields, who fronted the band, was deliberately sought out to complement Coppola's vision of the film by music producer Reitzell.[33] Shields also contributed two new compositions to the soundtrack, 'City Girl', which plays over the closing credits, and 'Are You Awake', of which more below.

A number of other pieces are employed to create cool, moody tones, particularly associated with the isolated experiences of Charlotte. Her first excursion into the city, starting on the subway, is accompanied by a composition by Reitzell and Roger J. Manning Jr: a low, slightly droning synthesiser, drum and piano piece that contributes to what appears to be the somewhat distanced and slightly puzzled nature of the character's engagement with her surroundings. Another gently moody piece, Sebastien Tellier's 'Fantino', with keyboard accompanied by background guitar, maintains the impression of separation or loneli-ness in a subsequent scene after Charlotte returns to her hotel room, in which she applies make-up, lies on her bed, hangs paper flowers on the ceiling and injures her toe. The music continues implacably, as is characteristic of each of these pieces, as if to signify a measure of detachment from the passage of events, marked here by the lack of any heightening of the moment at which Charlotte is hurt (the event is further distanced by occurring when she has her back to, and is on the far side of the bed from, the camera). A second synthesiser-led Reitzell and Manning track is used in the sequence at the Shibuya crossing, colder and more remote-seeming in its main emphasis. The chilliest of these pieces, unsurprisingly, is reserved for the extended pan towards and past Charlotte as she sits in her bedroom window, the glacial piano/synth tones of Squarepusher's 'Tommib', a simple repeated rising-and-falling higher pitch being accompanied by the development of a darker, lower tone. The piece is bleak, cold and fragile in its resonances, contributing directly and significantly to the impression of loneliness and vulnerability established in relation to the character. A return to the cool, distant 'moody' quality is found later in the Kyoto sequence, in 'Alone in Kyoto', composed for the film by Air, the group with which Coppola worked on *The Virgin Suicides*, a blend of elements of synthesiser and guitar that also includes some lighter touches of percussion.

The use of music in each of these sequences is clearly conventional in the extent to which it is closely related to the evocation of specific character experience at various stages in the development of the narrative. But the combination of sound and images seems in some of these instances to give them the status of audio-visual *set pieces*, even if relatively brief in duration, marked out as playing a more distinctive part in the establishment of the overall quality and positioning of the film. They can be understood as offering a particular variety of spectacle or attraction, terms usually associated with the special effects of mainstream Hollywood features (or performative forms of comedy, as indicated in the previous chapter), but which also seem to have some purchase here in suggesting one of the ways in which the film claims a particular place in both the cinematic and the wider taste-cultural spectrum.[34] This is, of course, a variety of spectacle or attraction that would be characterised in the kinds of terms highlighted in the previous section in relation to the visuals alone: 'subtle', 'nuanced' and the like, terms that might equally well be applied to the employment of music outlined above. As 'subtle' forms of attraction, sequences such as these might be less clearly marked off as separable components or as distinct 'highlights' of the film than some spectacular Hollywood set-pieces, even if they do offer a particular appeal that can function in a similar manner for the target audience.

Part of the measure of 'quality', in this region of the cinematic landscape, would usually be to favour a notion of integration, of the parts fitting smoothly into the whole, as opposed to any sense of the film being the outcome of an assemblage of separate components more cynically put together for more directly commercial reasons, which might include the more ostentatious display of set-pieces of one kind or another. Distinctions made along such lines between one kind of cinema and another are slippery, however, and always liable to over-simplification, although that is often the nature of these kinds of taste-cultural judgements (very many high-budget and/or spectacular Hollywood films are much more carefully and coherently constructed that is often suggested within these kinds of discourses, for example, while many examples of indie or art cinema offer forms of attraction of their own; the opposition between the two is often far less clear-cut than is sometimes implied[35]). The audio-visual set-pieces of *Lost in Translation* offer distinctive qualities, in their emphasis on the conveyance of mood more than of action or linear narrative development, but in a manner that remains closely integrated into the establishment of character and of some of the thematic dimensions considered in the next chapter. This is another respect in which the overall balance of qualities offered by the film can be understood via Klevan's examination of different degrees and *kinds* of eventfulness:

Although many films risk playing down plot elements or reduce urgent causality [as does *Lost in Translation*], they often substitute them with *eventful* 'interest in the visual' (or interest in the aural) [as also does *Lost in Translation* in its own way]: spectacular landscapes, arresting sound tracks, glamorous actors or the countless other visual and aural excitements or effects which the cinema can provide.[36]

As far as the music itself is concerned, the film appears to combine aspects of two opposed qualities suggested by Michel Chion, which might be another marker of the middle ground often occupied more broadly by the indie or Indiewood sectors.[37] Chion suggests that film music can be either 'empathetic' or 'anempathetic' in effect. In the former, the music directly expresses its participation in the scene while in the latter it exhibits 'conspicuous indifference to the situation, by progressing in a steady, undaunted, and ineluctable manner'.[38] The empathetic is what we would usually associate with Hollywood and other mainstream commercial cinemas; the anempathetic with the distanced strategies sometimes found in some works of art or indie cinema. The use of music in the sequences outlined above does seem to fulfil some of the qualities of the anempathetic, principally in its progression 'in a steady, undaunted, and ineluctable manner'. This is a key aspect of the distanced, alienated quality it often seems to evoke. But this is an alienation linked very directly to that of character, particularly Charlotte, which seems to make it more empathetic in general terms: the music invites the viewer to share vicariously some of the alienated or disoriented experience of the character. *Lost in Translation* is a melodrama in the literal sense of the term (melo-drama = music-drama), in which the music plays an important part in setting emotional tone. But another marker of the film's position is its general avoidance of devices associated more directly with the narrower use of the label to signify romantic or otherwise emotionally led films in which music is used in a more hyperbolic manner to chart the soaring and plunging trajectory of the emotional landscape (a feature of many Hollywood films beyond those traditionally allocated to the 'melodrama' genre, as several commentators have established[39]). This is partly the result of the kind of music used, as well as the ends to which it is deployed. The generally cool and distant nature of the non-diegetic music (that which is not generated from sources within the fictional world) is sufficient in itself to create an impression very different from that associated with classical instances of emotional melodramatic orchestration. The fact that the mood created is one that often reflects character distance, isolation or disorientation has a tendency to encourage a similar measure of cool distance on the part of the viewer, in contrast to the greater level of overt vicarious emotional participation urged by the musical rollercoaster effects associated with traditional melodrama. Emotional participation is far from being ruled out but is marked in this way as, again, more subtle, nuanced and less 'obvious' in character.

Coppola and Reitzell also refuse the option of using music to chart some of the more proximate emotional currents in the film. A small example is the absence of any response in the music to Charlotte's injury to her toe, as cited above. More significant, as a marker of distance from the dominant conception of 'melodrama', is the lack of any music in the preceding scene in which Charlotte sheds a quiet tear following her expression of concern about the nature of her relationship with John in a telephone call home. This is a moment that appears to be marked, quite specifically, as resisting the appeal of any melodramatic underpinning, whether more or less subtle in nature. Much the same goes for almost all of the sequences that mark the development of the relationship between Bob and Charlotte. Non-diegetic music is generally conspicuous by its absence (the same does not go for music that has diegetic sources, either in the bar or the karaoke scenes, which is considered below). The lengthy sequence in Bob's hotel bedroom is notably free of any musical accompaniment, more or less overt. In a sequence of such great importance to our understanding of where their relationship is or is not going, this is a significant absence. Music often functions in such instances (even if used with subtlety, as subtext or undertone) to provide guidance on the likely trajectory of development that might be expected. Not to use music to serve this purpose here is to extend the existing degree of uncertainty generated by the film about the extent to which it is or is not likely to bend in the direction of establishing a more conventional relationship between the two.

Non-diegetic music is in fact absent in large parts of the film, which tends to highlight the status of the sequences examined above as expressive set-pieces. The absence of music can be taken as another marker of the film's claim to the status of a certain degree of verisimilitude (of the 'objective' variety, as opposed to the subjective variant supported by the 'mood' music), a quality often seen as existing in opposition to the melodramatic. Ambient sound forms the background to many of the sequences in the hotel and elsewhere, including some more heightened examples that coincide with the use of hand-held camerawork. The verité impression created in the dash into the pachinko parlour is strongly underlined, for example, by the loud bleep, clatter and jangling of the machines, while the distance from the characters of the shot that captures their exit from the premises is equally marked by the sound perspective: the noise of the passing vehicles that obstruct our view of the figures across the road is relatively loud in the mix, clearly located in the aural foreground. A hubbub of street sounds also accompanies the moment at which Bob catches up with Charlotte for their final encounter on the street while on his way to the airport, although this is an example that demonstrates only a limited commitment to verité aesthetic at the level of sound. Street noise remains audible but significantly lowered in the mix once the pair enter their embrace, signifying perhaps their own mutual absorption in the moment but also the film's commitment to heightened matters of character emotion more than to its location in an entirely 'realistic' background context (in some indie features, noisy background sound continues to intrude in such instances, although that might be the result of technical/budgetary limitations as much as or more than any deliberate commitment to a particular aesthetic).

Music, both non-diegetic and diegetic, does also serve some purposes more directly related to narrative development than is found in the examples cited above. These include a number of anticipatory effects that foreshadow events to come, more and less overtly and with or without the use of direct points of reference in lyrics. An extract from 'The State We're In' by the Chemical Brothers performs an important function in the orchestration of Bob and Charlotte's first night out from the hotel. The piece begins briefly, quietly but with a promise to build towards a climax, when the former teases the latter as they leave after he picks her up from her room, creating a sound bridge to the nightclub scene in which its status shifts from non-diegetic to diegetic (a transition that constitutes an entirely conventional usage of music in mainstream cinema). The gentle initial chiming tones of the piece, with a soft, high-pitched vocal, seem well-matched to the light-hearted mood in which the pair depart. On the cut to the music playing at the club, it reaches what is characterised as a 'joyous' climax, a development in the music marked visually by the image of a giant balloon onto which starburst patterned lights are projected. The piece then returns to its 'developing' stage as it plays over shots in which a number of introductions are made between characters, maintaining a forward-momentum-developing beat that creates the impression of an extended introduction (although the extract actually comes towards the end of the original track), before again bursting to a climax with a cut to the light-patterned balloon. This is a much more upbeat use of music than the other examples considered so far and one that seems clearly motivated by its function of marking the quality of 'escape' that characterises the outing.

Another more strongly anticipatory quality is found in the use of 'Are You Awake?' by Kevin Shields in the jump-cut sequence in Charlotte's room. This, like the extract from 'The State We're In', is also faster and more upbeat than most of the non-diegetic music used in the film, a synthesiser-led piece that has a subtle but strong forward-driving quality that creates a impression of 'leading up to something', as the sequence does in its transition to the scenes shared by the protagonists in Bob's bedroom. It serves a direct purpose of narrative development, contributing significantly to the creation of an impression that something is going to happen in the ongoing progress of the relationship between the couple, even if it is not clear exactly what. This is an effect very different from the more general impression of drifting jet-lagged restlessness evoked elsewhere in the film. The music also serves here very fluently to smooth over any disjunction created by the employment of jump-cuts, or to create an overall impression in which the jump-cuts become part of the broader evocation of anticipation-leading-somewhere rather than of restlessness as a sustained state in its own right.

Diegetic music also serves some potentially more 'obvious' duties of narrative reinforcement or foreshadowing, via the lyrics of some of the songs that are sung either in the hotel bar or during the karaoke sequence. The first words we hear from the female lounge singer, before a series of cuts to other drinkers that leads us to Bob, are 'I'm in your arms and you are kissing me / But there seems to be something missing', which could be taken in retrospect as a distant foreshadowing of what we assume to have become only a one-night stand, and certainly a relationship for Bob in which something was missing. 'You stepped out of a dream', she intones at the start of another bar sequence, the one in which Charlotte reinforces her contact with Bob after being bored by the conversation of Kelly and the musician. This line is not played immediately over shots involving the connection between the pair, however, and the song retires quite distantly into the background in the remainder of the sequence, which makes it seem less evidently applicable to their situation, even if a 'dreamy' quality does characterise aspects of the film and, perhaps, something of what Charlotte might offer to Bob. A stronger impression of lyrical relevance might be felt in the last visit to the bar, when a male singer is at the piano (the other having at this stage gained too charged a role to be able to serve a background function in the same manner as before) and the focus is more exclusively on a close pairing of the central characters. 'When you walked into the room / There was voodoo in the vibes' starts to play over the couple looking closely at one another (with a cutaway to the singer in the middle). 'I was captured by your style / But I could not catch your eye' accompanies a pair of singles of each character followed by a return to the two-shot with which the sequence began, after which point the music is pulled into the background as they talk. Such lyrics could be read as functioning, in a very broad sense, to reinforce the status of their relationship, in keeping with a widespread tendency in more conventional romantic comedies to employ romantic standards as part of their generic infrastructure. It seems more likely, however, that they serve the opposite function, at least in part, marking the use of superficial romantic clichés against which the film is positioning itself, as it does in relation to some other aspects of conventional romantic narratives considered in the previous chapter. It is, perhaps, another indicator of the general stance of the film that they can work either way.

Apart from the generally unsympathetic and somewhat humorous characterisation of the two lounge singers and their rather fake-seeming and mannered styles of delivery (and the potential in-joke reference to Murray's *Saturday Night Live* equivalent), further grounds for reading these as negative reference points for the position occupied by the film itself are provided by the staging of the other major sources of lyrical narrative resonance: the numbers delivered by Bob and Charlotte during the karaoke session. References that are similarly applicable to the situation

Figure 22 'So special': potential character-reference in lyrical content, as Charlotte sings towards Bob. © 2003 Universal Studios

of the characters can be found here, although the context is very different. The nature of the engagement involved in these sequences is marked as 'sincere' and 'genuine', in contrast to the superficiality of the lounge singers, as suggested in Chapter 2. Some of the lyrical content also seems more 'honest' in nature. Elements of the lyrics of Charlotte's 'Brass in Pocket', sung partly but not exclusively in Bob's direction, could be taken to refer to aspects of her own relationship with him to which she cannot more directly give voice, including the demanding: 'I'm special, so special / I gotta have some of your attention / Give it to me', which might convey something of her privileged background and unspoken sense of superiority over the likes of John and Kelly (particularly, it might seem, in the light of Bob's later comment to her after the discovery of his assignation with the singer, when he replies to her jibes about his age with: 'Wasn't there anyone else there to lavish you with attention?'). Of more substantial resonance, perhaps, is the climactic lyric of 'More Than This' delivered by Bob, which could be taken as foreshadowing the realistic limitations imposed on the potential development of their relationship beyond the stage of briefly encountered friendship: 'More than this – you know there's nothing [looks at her] / More Than this [looks at her again] – tell me one thing / More than this – oooh there's nothing.' This appears to be a statement of harsh reality, underpinned by the sincere nature of the 'unprofessional' delivery, very different in tone from the clichés of the New York bar.

Some critics highlighted the significance of the music to *Lost in Translation*, but this was the case for only a minority of major US press reviews, many of which appear to include the qualities of the soundtrack within the kinds of broader phrases quoted in the previous section: general, mostly positive references to mood, atmosphere and style. Relatively untypical is the more direct, distinction-marking comment made in the *San Francisco Chronicle* that

the aural palette of 'Lost in Translation' is equally as important as its visual scheme. Apart from knowing when quiet is necessary, Coppola has impeccable taste in music and stocks her soundtrack with moody pieces that recall Brian Eno, and not the over-mixed power-pop ballads that flood so many studio movies.[40]

More passing appreciation is given in the *Boston Globe* to 'Coppola's knack for putting just the right French retro-rock tune on the soundtrack',[41] but none of the reviewers offers anything in the way of interpretation of the particular effects created by the use of music other than in consideration of the 'sincerity' of Murray's rendition of 'More Than This'. The latter is given some detailed consideration in *The New York Times*, a review that is unusual in devoting more general attention to the quality of sound in the film, followed by a name-check for the sound designer, Richard Beggs:

Sound is used so beautifully it takes your breath away; in a scene where Bob carries the dozing Charlotte to her room, the hotel corridor is gently dusted with aural density; the noise of air conditioners and fluorescent lights becomes a part of the milieu.[42]

Music is an important dimension of the film for some respondents in the Amazon sample, including the distinctive qualities of the indie outfits foregrounded on the soundtrack, but it figures in considerably fewer postings than visual style (and far fewer than narrative), which is perhaps not surprising given the priority that tends generally to be given to the visual dimension of audio-visual media such as film and television. Comments related to music, or to 'the soundtrack', are made by 143 out of the 1,900 respondents (7.5 per cent). Among these, the pattern has much in common with that relating to the visuals, a large majority making comments that are both positive (123; 6.4 per cent of the sample or 86 per cent of those commenting on the music/soundtrack) and brief in nature (110; 5.7 per cent or 76.9 per cent). Typical of these are the use of phrases such as 'great music', 'wonderful soundtrack' or 'very cool music', the bases of which remain unexpressed. The qualities of the music are the first point of reference in only two cases and are often commented upon in the latter stages of responses or as part of a list of positive attributes. In many cases, appreciation of sound and visuals is expressed jointly, as contributing to the mood or atmosphere created by the film. One refers to 'Sofia Coppola's recipe of vivid imagery and wonderfully ambient music' (ASH, Winston-Salem, NC, 27 June 2005) while another describes the film as 'an exquisite and unique amalgam of light, color, temporal rhythm, music, and emotion' (A Customer, 13 January 2004). As with the visuals, the dominant form of expression is brief and impressionistic, even where highly positive, with only seven respondents offering more detailed readings of how particular pieces of music work in specific sequences (a total of 25 postings cite particular bands or musicians by name, primarily Kevin Shields and/or My Bloody Valentine). The more detailed citations include the following:

The music selection fits perfectly with the atmosphere too. My Bloody Valentine is my favorite band, and their breathtaking song 'Sometimes' (as well as 4 other songs from the newly returned Kevin Shields . . . HELL YEAH!) played over the sparkling skyscrapers is the highlight of the film for me. (Kazuo, 8 July 2005)

The music was more than just a great score. It helped create and to generate the audiences [*sic*] emotions. As Charlotte gets on the train to visit the temple, the soft-rock playing lightly in the background represents how she is feeling at the time, upbeat and feel good. Then as she enters the temple, the soft-rock is faded-over with bell dongs, the beat of drums, and chanting from the monks. Lastly, the soft piano playing in the bar, as Bob and Charlotte poetically connect, is another example of the music complementing the films [*sic*] content. (PM Elam, 21 March 2005)

Negative responses are small in number, just seven (0.36 per cent of the total sample or 4.9 per cent of those who comment on this dimension of the film), ranging from the briefly dismissive – 'Music sucks' (A Customer, 4 October 2003) – to one that begins by complaining, somewhat oddly, that 'There is no soundtrack' ('thefly2385', Woodinville, WA United States, 17 March 2004). The only more specific negative view comes from one who finds the use of music excessive, referring to moments in which 'that damn music gets spread on too thick: Soft and tinkly one minute, loud and annoying the next' (A Customer, 24 February 2004). For those who appreciate the film overall, however, the music probably plays a significant part, even if its separate contribution to the formal texture of *Lost in Translation* is not always explicitly acknowledged in its own right.

4. Themes: Alienation, Disconnection and Representation

If we move on to ask what *Lost in Translation* is *about*, at the level of the themes with which it engages, explicitly or more implicitly, most apparent are the issues of loneliness, alienation and disconnection to which reference has already been made on numerous occasions in this book, including what is signified by some of the formal qualities examined in the previous chapter. The lack of overt narrative 'action', visuals such as the images of Charlotte framed in her hotel window or exploring parts of the city and the cooler tones of the soundtrack are all expressive of this dimension of the film, which is also one of its markers of positioning in relation to the tradition of art cinema. The jet-lagged Tokyo experiences of Bob and Charlotte, out of time and out of place, create a heightened expression of dislocation that seems intended to stand for a broader sense of alienation, a frequent subject of works of art cinema and other forms of cultural production that might be situated within either the modernist or postmodernist traditions (the alienating qualities of the city are strongly associated with certain strains within modernism that date back to the urban growth of the late nineteenth and early twentieth centuries, while the particular qualities of Tokyo neon and the hushed no-space of the hotel suggest a more obvious link with later accounts of the postmodern[1]). These issues are also closely linked to some aspects of the way the film can be read as offering a particular kind of representation of Japan and/or the Japanese, an area in which it has faced accusations of ethnic/racist stereotyping that imply a rather different cultural positioning.

During the period covered by the film, Bob and Charlotte are to some extent adrift from their usual moorings, existing in a state of limbo, between their pasts and futures. If this is marked as a space in which time is provided for reflection on the meaning and direction of their lives, it is not represented as something that leads clearly to any great insight, certainly not of a life-changing variety. On the one hand, the protagonists are assailed by an encompassing boredom and loneliness: in her case, what appear to be long hours alone in her hotel room pondering her future, or alienated from her husband and the company he keeps in relation to his work; in his, time spent mostly in propping up the bar while taking 'time out' from his family. On the other, there is the connection that becomes established, increasingly if perhaps fleetingly, between the two. It is possible to read aspects of this dimension of the film through a variety of theoretically or philosophically oriented perspectives, as an evocation of what might be interpreted as typically modern, postmodern or related experiences.[2]

Some of this material might be understood, for example, in terms of the quality of 'drift' associated by Leo Charney with modernity, in an account that draws on figures ranging from Marcel Proust to Walter Benjamin.[3] A key aspect of the modern experience for some of the thinkers cited by Charney is a loss of 'presence', of the possibility (probably always an illusion, however) of living more fully in the moment, an issue taken up directly in relation to *Lost in Translation*, although from a different direction, by Todd McGowan. For Charney, the emergence of cinema in the modern era offered the illusion of conquering the loss and 'absence' at the heart of modern existence.[4] McGowan praises *Lost in Translation* specifically as an evocation of absence, however, a quality declared in this reading, from a Lacanian psychoanalytical perspective, to be at the heart of all language, culture and subjectivity.[5] The enjoyment experienced by Bob and Charlotte, for McGowan, is based on their shared recognition of what the Lacanian perspective identifies as the fundamental absence and non-attainability of the privileged object of desire (the *objet petit a* in Lacan's terminology), a reading that requires the acceptance of a number of highly contestable Lacanian assumptions. The narrative slightness of the film and the fleeting nature of its evocation of Tokyo and the various experiences of the central characters is such that it would be easy to imagine readings of *Lost in Translation* from numerous such perspectives that have been influential in film theory in recent decades. It is the kind of film that lends itself to some such interpretations; or, put more critically, to a tradition in which films are sometimes used primarily as vehicles to illustrate pre-existing theoretical templates.[6]

How far such approaches are justified remains subject to debate and to the particular orientations of one analyst or another. As far as the dimensions of loneliness and alienation are concerned, in the manner in which they seem to be more clearly or immediately articulated by the film itself, rather than being reliant on the bringing to bear upon the text of heavy conceptual machineries, this is another dimension in which *Lost in Translation* might be judged to be relatively lightweight in its treatment, when compared with 'classics' such as the work of Antonioni in features such as *L'avventura*, *The Eclipse* (*L'eclissé*, 1962) and *The Red Desert* (*Il deserto rosso*, 1964) in which narrative drift is closely related to a stronger impression of alienation and/or dislocation. These are films of considerably heavier tone than *Lost in Translation*, their expressions of alienation more forcefully elaborated in relation to the textures of modern industrial or commercial landscapes, most explicitly in the case of *Il deserto rosso*.[7] By comparison, Coppola's work seems relatively slight, in keeping with its broader cultural and commercial positioning (one marker of difference can be seen in the contrast between the endings of *Lost in Translation* and Antonioni's *L'eclissé*: that of the former is warm and emotional, even if it ends in parting; that of the latter is the clearly distinct material of art-cinema modernism, a seven-minute montage sequence from which the two main characters remain absent after failing to make a planned assignation). The dimension of alienation is evoked most fully in relation to Charlotte's explorations of the city, along with her trip to Kyoto. The Japan through which she drifts is one that appears to be puzzling at almost all turns, but gently so, rather than posing what is presented as any real threat to her conception of self or the kind of anxiety suffered by Antonioni's central female protagonists (as are most of the encounters undergone by Bob, although his are narrower in range). One of the most notable features of this experience is that much the same seems to apply to the modern/postmodern/contemporary and the more traditional fabrics of Japan with which she engages.

The first expedition of Charlotte's to which we are witness takes her from the former to the latter; from subway and crowded streets to the quieter confines of a shrine in which she watches the monks performing their rites. The traditional ritual seems to offer no significant respite, however, as indicated implicitly by the continuing blankness of her expression and explicitly in her comment during her subsequent phone call home that 'I didn't feel anything'. A similar juxtaposition occurs later, when she wanders through the hotel in what appears to be an attempt to escape her boredom. First, she comes across Kelly giving her press conference, an event that might represent the epitome of postmodern media/celebrity-age superficiality, in its crass comments and

Figure 23 Celebrity superficiality: Kelly's press conference at the hotel. © 2003 Universal Studios

Figure 24 Traditional tranquility? Charlotte in the ikebana class. © 2003 Universal Studios

its relation to disposable, short-term popular cultural production. Next, she drifts into a room in which a woman in traditional kimono is leading an ikebana flower-arranging class, into which she is gently steered and encouraged to participate. This is a peaceful arena and an activity stereotypically associated with Japanese traditions of quiet, patience and order. It seems more positively coded by the filmmaker overall, but the experience is one from which Charlotte appears to remain more or less equally distanced. A similar sense of bemusement or distance, in relation to contrasting activities, is found in her subsequent witnessing of details including players in a Tokyo video-game arcade and a couple taking part in the formalities of a traditional wedding ceremony during her visit to Kyoto.

Broader issues relating to the expression of alienation or disconnection become implicated here in more specific questions about the representations of particular cultures, in this case prevailing western images of Japan. Some of the more pointed aspects of the latter will be examined below, but it is not possible to separate out central aspects of the general thematic dimension from the more nationally/culturally specific territory through which it is evoked. The nature of the experiences of Charlotte detailed above seems to buy into one key aspect of dominant western ideology, part of a series of Orientalist discourses that have historically been applied to this and other parts of the far east. The west has a long history of depicting Japan as a place of paradox and contradiction, as Ian Littlewood suggests, as a 'strange cultural mixture [. . .] of tradition and technology; refinement and brutality; east and west.'[8] Just such a mixture is suggested by the different facets of Tokyo/Japan drawn upon and implicitly contrasted by the film. The key to understanding an Orientalist discourse of this kind is that it tells us more about its source than it does about the overseas territories to which it is meant to refer.[9] The notion of paradox and contradiction is understood to be a product of the 'inherent peculiarity' of Japanese culture but is really a product of 'our own angle of vision'; that is to say, the 'paradox' only exists from a perspective in which such categories are separated out and made to be oppositional in the first place.[10] If the maintenance of such oppositions is an important part of western culture, as appears to be the case, it becomes necessary to define as paradoxical or contradictory any other culture in which the same kind of separation is not found. As Littlewood puts it:

To call Japan a paradox is really to say that it threatens the existing boundaries and therefore our definition of ourselves [and it is] for this reason that the language of paradox has always been counterbalanced by a language that reaffirms these boundaries as emphatically as possible.[11]

Lost in Translation seems here to be broadly complicit in a wider process of ideologically rooted western stereotyping, in the process of its articulation of the more specific alienation and disconnection suffered by the protagonists. There is one important component of the established mythology that it seems to avoid at least partially, however, in its portrayal of Charlotte as seemingly distanced from both the modern/ postmodern and the traditional. Certain aspects of Japanese culture – the tea-house and the Zen garden, or Buddhism more generally – have often been imagined in western culture as sources of tranquillity or spirituality, 'a dream of spiritual peace in the midst of modern urban pressures', as Littlewood puts it.[12] Spiritual peace of this kind is precisely what Charlotte might be seeking in her two temple or shrine visits, and what she might hope to have gained from her unplanned experience in the ikebana class. It is not to be found, however, a potential cliché that the film avoids at the level of narrative, although something of its texture is perhaps offered to the viewer in the tranquil nature of the pacing and audio-visual qualities that accompany the sequences in question (although how far these can be separated from those employed more widely in the film might be doubtful, reducing the extent to which they might distinctly fulfil such a purpose in these specific instances). The film seems in this case quite clearly to invest in the more general notion of alienation/disconnection rather than in the territory-specific mythology of Japanese tradition as source of solace, although it seems to be the overlap between these two dimensions that results in some of its problems for viewers who complain about racial stereotyping.

The role of Tokyo, Japan and the Japanese in *Lost in Translation* is largely to serve as a backcloth against which to set the situations of and developing relationship between the two central characters. The city (along with the country more generally and those of its people who are represented) is structurally located as 'other' to the protagonists, a position from which some degree of reductive stereotyping easily results. Tokyo/Japan/Japanese serves as the primary signifier – although not the only one, as suggested below – of the 'alien' world within which Bob and Charlotte feel abandoned and eventually find one another. The issue then becomes the manner in which this world is presented and the grounds on which the difference between it and that of the protagonists is marked. It is possible to signify 'difference' in a non-reductive or non-stereotypical way, but this is not something Coppola seems to achieve, certainly not in some parts of the film. A good deal of the comedy offered by *Lost in Translation* seems to rely on rather cheap and obvious stereotypes, in a manner that is somewhat surprising and out of tune with its broader positioning in the film-cultural landscape. A number of verbal jokes are based around the tendency of Japanese characters to render what should be 'r' sounds as 'l' sounds, examples of which have been cited in the previous chapters ('lip' instead of 'rip' my stockings; 'Loger' instead of 'Roger' Moore; 'brack' instead of 'black' toe, etc.). A similar number of visual jokes relate to the diminutive stature of many Japanese people, some of which do not seem to make much sense other than as arbitrary mocking. Bob bends uncomfortably to get beneath a shower head that is fixed too low and apparently cannot be adjusted sufficiently upwards, for example, although the pole to which it is attached seems to have plenty of further height capacity (and it seems unlikely that a luxury hotel would have facilities incapable of catering for taller guests). Likewise, he attempts to shave with a tiny complimentary razor, when it would seem implausible that such a character would not carry his own of more suitable size. The lack of any other motivation for such examples makes them appear to be egregious cases of crude stereotyping, in search of cheap laughs. The film also has a tendency to emphasise the 'crazy' or 'extreme' nature of some aspects of Japanese culture, including the 'premium fantasy' prostitute who visits Bob in his hotel room and the oddball chat-show host with whom Bob appears on television, among several others. There are some more 'normal'-seeming Japanese characters, principally some of those with whom Bob and Charlotte socialise on their first night of escape from the hotel, although their nature seems in this context to be shaped by their background function in relationship to the particular experience undergone at the time by the protagonists rather than being given any space to exist in its own right.

These and other aspects of what are seen as racist or otherwise negative stereotypes led to reported concerns by local distributors about how the film was likely to be received in Japan.[13] They were also noted by some Japanese critics when the film opened in Tokyo. A review in *Yomiuri Shimbun*, the country's largest-circulation daily, described Coppola's portrait of Japan as 'outrageously biased and banal'.[14] At home, a campaign against *Lost in Translation* was waged by Asian Mediawatch, which urged members of the Academy of Motion Picture Arts and Sciences to vote against the film in the Oscars.[15] Questions about potential racial stereotyping were also raised in a number of US press reports before and after the release of the film, although not in most of the review coverage.[16] This dimension of the film also draws criticism from some respondents in the Amazon sample, although a third of those who comment on the issue come to the opposite conclusion and seek to acquit the film of any such charges. A total of 199 of the 1,900 make reference to the issue (10.47 per cent of the sample), of whom 121 respond negatively (6.36 per cent of the total or 60.8 per cent of those who take up the subject). Most of these comment relatively briefly, describing the film variously as 'racist', 'stereotypical' and/or 'offensive', or accuse it of failing to offer any developed Japanese characters. One begins with reference to Edward Said's *Orientalism*, wondering why so few critics noticed 'that the film is literally overflowing with the racist clichés that Said identified as lying at the heart of so much of the West's interpretations of Eastern culture' (T. N. Parsons, Sydney, Australia, 28 November 2004), while another response is headlined 'Welcome back Orientalism', without any reference to Said by name (A Customer, 7 December 2003).

Some Amazon respondents argue that the film is more even-handed; that satire is directed at aspects of both Japanese culture and that of the visiting Americans. One suggests that those who complain about anti-Japanese sentiment are missing the point: 'The two characters, Bob in particular, are very real clichés of the ugly American. Rather than taking Coppola to task for making fun of Japanese people, I give her credit for showing us ourselves' (Steve, Las Vegas, 1 June 2008). A number of those who come to Coppola's defence (a total of 67; 33.68 per cent of those who comment on the issue), often responding to accusations made in the same forum, do so on the basis of the function of the Japanese background in relation to the themes of alienation or disconnection examined above: 'So Coppola's treatment of Japanese characters isn't racist or demeaning. It is just a plot device used to emphasise how Charlotte and Bob are feeling' (Jonathan B Whitcombe, New Hampshire USA, 21 March 2005). Among twelve respondents who identify themselves as Japanese or Japanese-American, the response is positive by a majority of eight to four, one expressing disgust at a film 'filled with racism and ignorance' (Ichiyo Higuchi, Tokyo, Japan, 14 February 2005) while another describes the film as 'full of shrewd observations about current Japanese culture . . . without resorting to stereotypes' (Ed Uyeshima, San Francisco, CA USA, 14 August 2004).

It is certainly the case that elements of Tokyo, Japan or the Japanese are not the only 'others' against which the positions occupied by Bob and Charlotte are defined. The other obvious example is the world of 'superficial' pop culture and action cinema signified by Kelly and John. This is likely to be a more comfortable object of negative reference for the principal target market of the film than jokes based around stereotypes of Japanese people; the latter is one dimension in which the film seems to be at its most mainstream in orientation. Other aspects of American or western culture are also subjected to implicit forms of mockery, including the lounge singers, the two businessmen who attempt to engage Bob in conversation on his first night and Bob's own 'mid-life crisis' as identified by Charlotte. A kind of parallel to any 'spiritual' insight Charlotte might hope to have gained from Buddhism is provided by the American self-help recording to which she listens, 'A Soul's Search', with its earnestly nonsensical-sounding 'inner map theory', although it is not quite clear how seriously she is meant to be taking it (we witness her listening to it on more than one occasion). With the exception of Kelly or John and background characters with whom they are located, any humour directed at representatives of American/western culture is implicit and low-key, however. Among the westerners, one grouping is separated off and less positively marked, while little such distinction appears to be made among the Japanese characters, which does suggest a basic structural lack of even-handedness in the film. Discrimination is made more clearly *between* Americans while most Japanese are presented as objects for the amusement of the viewer.

Another, less immediately obvious racial dimension of the film is the characterisation of Charlotte in particular as distinctly 'white', in the manner in which the category is analysed by Richard Dyer.[17] A very specific cultural construct with no innate existence in reality, whiteness of skin colour is often taken within western discourses to be a neutral, unmarked term, that of a universal human norm against which others are distinguished, a basis for a whole history of racist and imperialist inscriptions. At the centre of these, for Dyer, is the image of the white woman as an embodiment of notions of 'purity', a complex into which the figuration of Charlotte can be seen implicitly to play. Her complexion, as manifested by Johansson, is markedly pale, a significant component of the manner in which the character is established as 'fresh', young and, in some respects, innocent, in contrast to the pock-marked 'lived-in' face of Bob/Murray; her face tends to emit a soft, muted glow, usually in low-contrast lighting, while the paleness of her skin is further emphasised in the numerous sequences in which she inhabits her hotel room while only partially clad (an issue to which we return below).

The racial connotations of the manner in which Charlotte is presented as markedly white/pure operate at an underlying, structural level of which the filmmaker would not generally be expected to be aware; the aim of Dyer's intervention is, precisely, to bring this to attention, a project that involves 'making whiteness strange' and recognised as a

Figure 25 'White' bodily display: Charlotte, in characteristic semi-dressed mode (listening to the 'inner map' theory). © 2003 Universal Studios

culturally powerful construction rather than something taken to be invisible and somehow 'natural'.[18] The more obviously apparent negative stereotyping of Japanese characters does not appear to have been the intention of Coppola either. Those who have sought to defend Coppola on the charge in the media tend to make much of her love for and experience of living in the country.[19] It is not necessary for any intentionality to be involved, however, for representations to have potentially reductive stereotypical implications, either in the more obvious territory of the sources of humour detailed above or broader elements of consonance with Orientalist or other racially oriented discursive structures. Gender is another factor that can be added to the mix, both in itself and its relationship with questions of Orientalism. A specific gendered position can offer particular inflections of Orientalist discourses, as Reina Lewis argues in her study of the creative output of women in relation to nineteenth-century European imperialism.[20] In her analysis of the work of the French artist Henriette Browne, for example, Lewis finds 'a feminized version of the Orient', rooted in the contradictory enunciative positions occupied by women within Orientalism: superior in the divisions of colonialism but placed as other and inferior in the gendered divides of European art and society.[21] The result, Lewis stresses, is not necessarily a form of representation more truthful or non-imperialist than those produced by men, but something in which the 'mixture of observation and fantasy about the East is specifically gendered' as a result of their social location.[22] Can something akin to this be said in relation to any dimensions of Coppola's *Lost in Translation?*

The socially situated position of a woman filmmaker such as Coppola is different in some respects from that of male counterparts, not the least in finding it far more difficult in general to get projects off the ground, a recurrent problem for women operating in the independent sector as well as in the Hollywood mainstream (many have faced particular difficulty in gaining the support necessary to follow up an indie debut, even a successful one, with a second feature, as was achieved by Coppola in this instance[23]). How far such a difference might translate into an identifiably different type of filmmaking is more controversial territory, as is the question of whether or not clearly gender-based differences can be established in other forms of art and/or culture. Feminist theorists have engaged in numerous arguments about the existence or nature of a distinctly female-gendered perspective in the cinema, often in connection with psychoanalytically oriented approaches that dominated this realm of film analysis in the latter decades of the twentieth century. Judith Mayne, for example, associates the work of women filmmakers with an emphasis on female relationships, distinct conceptions of 'female desire' and, ultimately, what seems to be a lesbian orientation.[24] Such perspectives tend to share with that of McGowan considered above a requirement for the more or less wholesale acceptance of considerable bodies of psychoanalytical theory, of one school or another, which renders them at the very least questionable and subject to (probably endless) debate.[25]

Aspects of a film such as *Lost in Translation* can also be related to gender in some more proximate and concrete terms, however, although these also need qualification. Key elements of the film might be described as displaying what would be seen as a female more than a male perspective according to prevailing social-cultural assumptions, in dimensions such as its gentle tones and its favouring of subtle moments of character observation and the creation of atmospherics over strongly forward-moving action and event, the latter of which might be understood in some ways as being more consonant with more goal-oriented dominant western male gender constructions.[26] To say that such qualities might have some fit, broadly, with socio-culturally based constructions of gender does not seem unreasonable, although it would be quite another step to suggest that these might in any way be exclusively the preserve of women filmmakers, particularly given the wider provenance some such textual qualities have had in the indie or art cinema sectors (what might, from one perspective, be seen as a gender-based difference might, from another, be related to different positions in the cinematic spectrum that are available to filmmakers of any gendered position). Whether these more 'female'-oriented qualities might apply specifically to the Orientalist or otherwise racially stereotypical dimensions of the film is considerably less clear. The modality in which much of the stereotype-based humour is deployed is also relatively quiet and subtle in many cases, a matter of low-key misunderstandings and momentary confusions in the linguistic instances, but some of the humour itself is marked as crude and 'obvious' in a manner that seems less likely to be associated with a distinctly female or otherwise specifically gendered perspective.

In some dimensions *Lost in Translation* could be interpreted as a more conventional product of patriarchal culture, regardless of the details of individual authorship. The conjunction of a conventionally attractive younger woman and a much older male is a familiar ingredient of patriarchal assumptions, even if this occurs within a relationship in which companionship is favoured over romance or sexuality. The fact that Charlotte spends considerable stretches of the film dressed skimpily, with only underwear on her lower half, an issue addressed in relation to the opening sequence at the start of this book, might be part of the manner in which the vulnerability of the character is figured, but the result is a display of the female body that would be likely to be viewed as blatantly sexist had the filmmaker been male (the same might be said of the sequence in the sex bar from which Charlotte and Bob begin their second night of escape in the city, despite the fact that it is a venue from which the principals are clearly distanced). The body of Charlotte/ Scarlet is offered as a pleasurable form of visual spectacle, even if one that is also coded in aspects of dress and deportment as 'classy' and relatively 'upmarket', much in tune with the cultural positioning sought by the film itself (her body is also a few degrees more fleshy than conventional standard of 'perfection' associated with Hollywood images). This could be read as a more 'subtle' middle-class-oriented version of what might elsewhere be taken to be crude objectification. A rather negatively coded long-distance aural portrait is given of Bob's wife, with whom we might be encouraged to have sympathy in some respects but whose structural role for much of the film is generally as a representative of the imprisoning nature of long-term domesticity. This is another familiar patriarchal trope even if a somewhat more complex portrait results from Bob's comments to Charlotte about the joys as well as the restrictions resulting from paternity. Some balance is provided in the gender equation, as far as the critical portrait of character is concerned. Some of the foibles of Bob are also implicitly questioned by the film, especially in his dalliance with the singer, and John is another male character given generally unflattering characterisation, largely via his affinity with the pop cultural world of Kelly. The balance of attention devoted by the film to the male and female leads is more even than is sometimes the case in mainstream productions, especially given the greater star-capital possessed by the former, but the more overt gender politics of *Lost in Translation* is another dimension in which contrary pulls seem to exist between the more and less mainstream/conventional ends of the spectrum.

Much the same could be said of how the film might be interpreted from the position of a class-based politics. If it aims to be, in part, a study of contemporary alienation, disconnection and the remaining potential for the forging of personal relationships, this is all carried out within a very privileged arena. The primary setting in a luxury hotel and the material comfort of the central characters might be intended to create the space to focus on wider or more 'universal' aspects of experience, but it is questionable how far this is the case. The background world of the film might better be described as one of well-heeled upper bourgeois/individualistic complacency, with much less to say about the social realities of life and relationships as they are likely to be lived by anyone with a greater resemblance to the normalities of existence for the majority, or particularly for those who exist closer to the margins (a number of Amazon respondents note, for example, their lack of interest in the character of Charlotte, who they view as a spoilt rich kid; the particular character of the pale-skinned qualities examined above also suggests a specific kind of class positioning). There is scope to read aspects of the film as an implicitly more critical portrait of the alienating textures of contemporary capitalist/consumer society, but the emphasis of this dimension seems to be on broader notions of disconnection rather than on anything that lends itself very readily to a more politically radical interpretation.[27]

This is another quality *Lost in Translation* shares with the examples of European art cinema cited above, which can be related directly to the commercial positions of such work in the cultural-taste spectrum. *Lost in Translation* is not a film designed (consciously or otherwise) for the larger reaches of the mass market, but to appeal to particular substantial-niche constituencies the self-definitions of which are likely to include a considerable measure of distance from what is perceived to be the most popular end of the spectrum, as reflected in the acts of cultural discrimination performed within the text. It is, ultimately, a distinctly bourgeois product, designed to appeal to specific sectors of the middle-class audience, those in possession of the requisite cultural capital to find pleasure in the particular aesthetic and other qualities examined in the previous two chapters. And it seems to be this dimension that is given priority in the overall stance of the film. Its positioning in the cultural-taste spectrum, with the particular mixture of points of distinction and relatively more mainstream elements that is considered throughout this study, seems to override any real concern about issues of representation that have implications at the level of ethnicity, gender or anything else. This seems to be the level at which the film is most clearly self-defined and marked out, rather than, say, as specifically the product of a woman filmmaker or someone with a particular stance in relationship to the broader urban-capitalist or more specific Japanese setting, which is why these are the dimensions to which I have devoted most attention in this book.

Afterword

On balance, where exactly, then, does *Lost in Translation* sit in the wider independent/Indiewood spectrum? There is, perhaps, no single or one-dimensional answer. Some aspects of the film lean towards the Indiewood pole, particularly at the industrial level and in the centrality of a major star such as Bill Murray both to the film itself and the manner in which it was sold. More distinctly indie qualities also remain to the fore, however, and play a central part in establishing the particular resonances of the film, notably in the formal dimension, most obviously the low-key nature of its narrative framework. As much as anything, though, I would argue that the kind of close analysis of the various dimensions of the film conducted above demonstrates the different degrees in which qualities associated with the indie sector are often found, either more broadly or within an individual example such as this.

It is possible to suggest an overall leaning towards a particular kind of balance between the relatively mainstream-conventional and the relatively distinctive, as I have sought to do in detail in each of the chapters of this book. *Lost in Translation* can quite clearly be distinguished from both the core Hollywood mainstream, on the one hand (even if that remains itself a less one-dimensional phenomenon than is sometimes suggested), and the more alternative or lower-budget end of the indie spectrum, on the other (itself subject to numerous variations). The hybrid space it occupies is distinctive in its own ways, and became a significant part of the American film landscape from the late 1990s and into the 2000s, but remains far from monolithic in its own qualities or in the nature of its potential appeal to viewers.

Notes

Introduction

1 Bourdieu, 1993.

2 For more on these questions of definition, see introduction to King, 2005, and Tzioumakis, 2006.

3 See introduction to King, 2009, which offers a lengthy consideration of these issues and some of the underlying theories involved. The concept of the implied audience is from Barker and Austin, 2000, pp. 42–8. The classic work on the notion of cultural capital, and the taste-cultural preferences of different social groups, is Bourdieu, 1984.

4 A number of caveats have to be issued with the use of such samples, however. They are self-selecting and there is no guarantee that they are representative, although the Amazon sample is substantial and includes a range of responses, primarily from the United States but also with a wider geographical spread. I chose to use Amazon reviews as the principal source of viewer responses on the basis that the online retailer was likely to include as wide a range of viewers as any other sample. The sample from the IMDb has not been examined in the same detail, although it does appear to contain many similar currents of opinion.

Chapter 1

1 Details from various articles and interviews with Coppola, especially Thompson, 2003. Also see Diaconescu, 2001. Online sources cited here and elsewhere in this book were accessed at various times between September 2007 and May 2009.

2 Diaconescu, 2001.

3 Ribisi appears to confirm the connection in Meyer, 2003.

4 Thompson, 2003.

5 Hundley, 2003.
6 As widely reported in interviews with Coppola and other press reports, including some of those cited above.
7 Thompson, 2003.
8 Thompson, 2003; Harris, 2003.
9 Thompson, 2003.
10 King, 2005.
11 Thompson, 2003.
12 Thompson, 2003.
13 'Guerrilla style' in Diaconescu, 2001; 'run and gun' and 'Dogme-style' in Thompson, 2003, the latter a reference to the Danish Dogme 95 movement, which included a list of prohibitions that claimed a greater commitment to realism in filmmaking; 'documentary style' quotation from Coppola in Mitchell, W., 2003.
14 Thompson, 2003.
15 Details, variously, from Thompson, 2003, Mitchell, W., 2003, and Acord, 2004. See also the 'Lost on Location' feature provided as an extra on the DVD release.
16 Thompson, 2003.
17 Acord, 2004.
18 Harris, 2003.
19 Grove, 2003b; Thompson, 2003.
20 Hirschberg, 2003.
21 Crabtree, 2003.
22 For this and the above detail, see Harris, 2003, and Harris and Dunkley, 2003.
23 Bing, 2003.
24 I am drawing here on my previous accounts of Focus in King, 2004 and King, 2009
25 For more detail see Wyatt, 1998.
26 Grove, 2003a. The *New York Times* magazine piece is Hirschberg, 2003.
27 Harris, 2003.
28 Grove, 2003a.
29 Grove, 2003a.
30 For more on this, see King, 2009, chapter 1.
31 Snyder, 2004.
32 These and the following details are from Variety Staff, 2003.
33 Brooks, 2003a.
34 Brooks, 2003a.

35 Brooks, 2003b.
36 *Dummy* figures from the Internet Movie DataBase, www.imdb.com; week-by-week summary of *Lost in Translation* release, weekend gross and per-theatre average available in Anomymous and undated, 'Lost in Translation', 'Projects' listings, *The Hollywood Reporter*, accessed at www.hollywoodreporter.com/hr/tools_data/projects/project_display.jsp?pid=154560.
37 Grove, 2003a.
38 Grove, 2003a.
39 Details of weekend openings, box office, numbers of engagements and other data accessed from *Variety* tables searchable by date, starting at www.variety.com/index.asp?layout=b_o_weekend&dept=Film.
40 Overseas box office figure as reported by www.boxofficemojo.com.
41 Figures from entries for individual films on the Internet Movie DataBase, www.imdb.com.
42 Grove, 2004a.
43 For more detail, see 'Lost in Translation', 'Projects' listings (n. 36).
44 Grove, 2004b.
45 One such experiment, the Film Movement, was launched in 2002 by Larry Meistrich, in which some films would be available on DVD by subscription at the same time that they went on limited theatrical release.
46 Hettrick, 2004. The DVD rental figure is from a Saccone, 2004. I have been unable to locate total DVD revenue figures for the film, such data generally being less accessible than box-office data.
47 Hettrick, 2004.
48 Hettrick, 2004.
49 Mitchell, E., 2004.
50 For more on this see King, 2004.
51 I make much the same argument in the more detailed consideration of Focus strategies in King, 2009, chapter 5.
52 'Focus Reel' is found under the 'About Focus' heading at www.focusfeatures.com, although updated with new film titles over time.
53 Mitchell, E., 2003.
54 Turan, 2003.
55 Lumenick, 2003.
56 Clark, M., 2003.
57 Zacharek, 2003.
58 The 95 per cent positive rating placed the film only in equal 18th place for the year in the Rotten Tomatoes rankings, but with a far larger total

number of reviews than most of those placed more highly. For details of the nature of the sample of reviews used by the site, and the criteria for inclusion, see www.rottentomatoes.com/help_desk/faq.php.

59 Metacritic weights reviews in favour of those considered to be from more influential critics, although it gives no detail of how exactly the weighting works. See www.metacritic.com/about/scoring.shtml.

60 Amazon reviews accessed 13 August 2008, via www.amazon.com. The total listed by Amazon at this time was 1,919, which I reduced to 1,900 after removing a number of apparent duplicates and some that were not about the film at all.

61 Accessed 16 September 2008.

Chapter 2

1 'Articulating Stardom', in King, B., 1991. I discuss these concepts further in King, 2002b, chapter 5.

2 For more on this see King, 2002a, chapter 1. Essays on this topic can be found in Karnick and Jenkins, 1995.

3 For the classic account, see Seidman, 1979 and readings in relation to a number of other performers in King, 2002a.

4 For more on comedy as a modality, see King, 2002a, introduction. On the concept of implication, see Purdie, 1993. On allegiance, see Smith, 1995.

5 Examples of journalistic profiles that include a sense of this career shift include Brownfield, 2004. Scott, 2003; Hirschberg, 1999; Elder, 2001; uncredited, 'Bill Murray' entry on www.wikipedia.org.

6 For more examples of this kind of framing, see King 2002a, chapter 1.

7 Kael review in *The New Yorker*, cited by Brownfield, 2004; Elder, 2001.

8 See, for example, Hirschberg, 2003 and Scott, 2003, each published before or the week of the opening of the film.

9 I have kept the form of identification and location used by Amazon respondents themselves, even where this results in some inconsistencies in style, along with any other quirks of writing or punctuation. Respondents who choose not to give their identity are given the generic Amazon category 'A Customer'.

10 For examples from the press coverage of 2003, see Clark, J., 2003; Heffernan, 2003.

11 Sarris, 1981.

12 Sarris, 1981, p. 64.

13 As David Bordwell suggests, the 'classical' Hollywood style offers a number of options regarding the formal devices that might be used to achieve particular effects, creating scope for individuals to make their mark through consistent patterns of choices within the dominant paradigm; see Bordwell, 1985, pp. 77–82.

14 For a flavour of some of the circle surrounding Coppola, see Hirschberg, 2003. For a different take on the importance of such networks, see De Vany, 2004, p. 239. De Vany argues that, in an industry characterised by short-term organisation of skilled workers, the existence and development of such connections can play a significant part in increasing the opportunities for the creative artist, a reading that seems particularly appropriate in the case of Sofia Coppola.

15 Rooney, 2003; Honeycutt, 2003.

16 Mitchell, 2003.

17 Turan, 2003.

18 Lumenick, 2003.

19 Clark, M., 2003. Other critics who make no reference to *The Virgin Suicides* include Ebert, 2003 and Burr, 2003.

20 Caro, 2003.

21 Axmaker, 2003.

22 Hohenadel, 2006.

23 Siegel, 2009.

24 Coppola was also co-director, with Andrew Durham and Ione Skye, of an earlier short film, *Bed, Bath and Beyond* (1996), a film less often mentioned in accounts of her early career and one I have been unable to view at the time of writing.

25 Mitchell, 2003.

26 For more on this see King, 2005, chapter 4.

27 For more on this and other conventional aspects of romantic comedy, see King, 2002a, pp. 50–62. On some more recent examples, see essays in Evans and Deleyto, 1998.

28 One classic example of this variety is *Bringing Up Baby* (1938).

29 In some of the less conventional Hollywood varieties, including *My Best Friend's Wedding* (1997), friendship outside the central couple is offered as an alternative source of emotional bonding; see 'Introduction: Surviving Love', in Evans and Deleyto, 1998.

30 For example, *You've Got Mail* (1998).

31 For examples see King, 2002a, pp. 57–61.

32 For more on this see King, 2005, pp. 187–9. For analysis of another Indiewood example, also distributed by Focus Features, see my reading of *Eternal Sunshine of the Spotless Mind* in King, 2009 chapter 1.

33 For an acknowledgement of the connection with *Lost in Translation* by the film's director, Pen-ek Ratanaruang, see Hale, 2004.

34 The quotation relating to *Last Life in the Universe* is attributed to *The Big Issue*; Honeycutt, 2006.

35 The depiction of urban decadence provided by Fellini is significantly more challenging than the presence of any such elements in *Lost in Translation*, however, sustaining a more alienated and unsentimental portrait of its central character.

36 For other examples see Amazon responses cited in King, 2009 and King 2007.

Chapter 3

1 For more on each of these tendencies, see King, 2005, chapter 2.

2 This way of understanding how narrative might be read by viewers, also employed in the previous chapter, is based upon an inferential model of narration, as proposed by David Bordwell, according to which the spectator is understood perceptually to process representational material and to elaborate its meaning on the bases of available schemes such as those provided by dominant narrative, genre and other frameworks; see Bordwell, 2008.

3 All timings are taken from those given on the region 1 DVD release.

4 The three-act structure is the basis of Hollywood narrative structure taken as a given in the majority of screenwriting manuals. For an argument in favour of a four-part version, see Thompson, 1999. For a useful overview, see Bordwell, 2006, pp. 28–42.

5 Bordwell, 2008, p. 120.

6 Bordwell, 1985a, chapter 10.

7 Bordwell, 1985a, p. 207.

8 Bordwell, 1985a, p. 207.

9 Bordwell, 1985a, p. 208.

10 Klevan, 2000. As Klevan observes, many 'classic' instances of art cinema often associated with 'realism' remain focused around instances of crisis of one kind or another rather than really seeking to evoke something closer to 'ordinary' or 'everyday' experience.

11 Klevan, 2000, p. 108.

12 Bordwell, 1985a, p. 212.
13 See, for example, Block, 2008, p. 237.
14 Bordwell, 2008, p. 141.
15 Bordwell, 2008, p. 122. According to my calculation, the ASL for *Lost in Translation* is 6.526 seconds: a total of 878 shots in 95 minutes, 30 seconds (5,730 seconds), from the end of the opening company credits to the fade-to-black that precedes the end credits.
16 An example of the latter suggested by Bordwell is *13 Conversations about One Thing* (2001), which has an ASL in the 10–11-second range. A similar figure is recorded for Steven Soderbergh's remake of *Solaris* (2002), however, demonstrating the possibility of higher ASL figures in the Indiewood realm; for more on *Solaris*, see King, 2009, chapter 3.
17 Bordwell, 2006, p. 140.
18 For more on Jost, see King, 2005, chapter 3.
19 For more on this film also, see King, 2005. And it is worth noting that even here, in a much more art-cinema-oriented indie feature, such formal departures are generally motivated by the state of mind of the central character.
20 Mitchell, E., 2003.
21 Burr, 2003.
22 Guthmann, 2003; Axmaker, 2003.
23 Zachurek, 2003.
24 Bordwell, 2006, p. 189. Heightened usages of intensified continuity exist, in Bordwell's account, alongside more modest employments of similar stylistic devices.
25 Bourdiey, 1984.
26 Barker and Brooks, 1998, p. 157.
27 King, 2009, introduction.
28 For a prominent example of a critical tradition that explicitly valorises subtlety as a marker of aesthetic quality, without any consideration of the broader socio-cultural basis of the distinction upon which it is based, see Perkins, 1972.
29 Bordwell, 2006, p. 62.
30 Bourdieu, 1993, p. 39.
31 Hundley, 2003.
32 For more on the qualities associated with indie music, which include many striking overlaps with those associated with indie film, see Fonarow, 2006.
33 Hundley, 2003.

34 I am using the term 'attraction' here in the more general sense of stand-out appealing elements rather than with the specific political dimensions included in its employment by Tom Gunning in his classic account of early cinema (see Gunning, 1990).

35 On the Hollywood side, see King, 2000, King, 2002b, chapter 6, and Bordwell, 2006; on the use of formally based attractions in indie cinema, see King, 2005, pp. 148–58.

36 Klevan, 2000, p. 63. The quoted phrase 'interest in the visual' is from Stanley Cavell.

37 Chion, 1994.

38 Chion, 1994, p. 8.

39 See, in particular, Neale, 2000, pp. 3–4, 179–205.

40 Guthmann, 2003.

41 Burr, 2003.

42 Mitchell, E., 2003.

Chapter 4

1 See, for example, Kern, 2003 and Harvey, 1991.

2 To suggest that some of the thematic dimensions of *Lost in Translation* might be read as an evocation of such experiences is not to imply that the film embodies modernist or postmodernist qualities in itself. In my reading, the film is some considerable distance from being either a modernist or a postmodernist text, its departures from mainstream convention being insufficient to merit the attachment of either label, however contested each might be.

3 Charney, 1998.

4 Charney, 1998, p. 42.

5 McGowan, 2007.

6 For another example, in this case a use of the film as a vehicle for an essay on the film theory of Gilles Deleuze, see Colman, 2005.

7 For more detail about Antonioni and the place of such films in the canon of art cinema, see Kolker, 1982, pp. 142–6. See also Kovács, 2007. The latter offers a number of useful distinctions between works of art cinema that fulfil the characteristics of modernist art and those which remain closer to the 'classical' cinematic tradition, as might be the case with *Lost in Translation*.

8 Littlewood, 1996, p. 7.

9 The classic account is Said, 1978.

10 Littlewood, 1996: 8.
11 Littlewood, 1996, p. 8.
12 Littlewood, 1996, p. 87.
13 Rich, 2004.
14 Quoted in Musetto, 2004.
15 Wright, 2004.
16 For an account that includes a Japanese perspective, mostly critical, see
    Rich, 2004. A more sympathetic account, in which Coppola's represen-
    tations of Japan are described as 'far removed from traditional stere-
    otypes', is found in Cheng, 2003. A British example of strong criticism is
    Day, 2004.
17 Dyer, 1997.
18 Dyer, 1997, p. 4.
19 For one such positive interpretation of the film, in the context of journal-
    istic account of images of Japan in American cinema, see Cheng, 2003.
20 Lewis, 1996.
21 Lewis, 1996, pp. 127, 4–5.
22 Lewis, 1996, p. 184.
23 For examples, see King, 2005, pp. 223, 226.
24 Mayne, 1990.
25 Another example is Bainbridge, 2008. Bainbridge argues that various
    qualities in a group of art-cinema leaning films can be seen as expressions
    of aspects of 'feminine' experience explored in the particular psychoana-
    lytically rooted theories of Luce Irigaray. An Irigarayan reading of *Lost
    in Translation* is made in Bolton, 2006. Bolton offers some useful observa-
    tions about the manner in which the film offers space for the exploration
    of the subjectivity of Charlotte, but it is far from clear that the Irigarayan
    framework is necessary for such points to be made. Bolton's account also
    treats the film as if it exists in isolation from the tradition of art cinema in
    relation to which the qualities on which she focuses need to be situated
    if they are to be understood in context.
26 For other examples of such qualities in independent productions from
    women filmmakers, see King, 2005, pp. 226–7.
27 For a different interpretation, however, see McGowan, who interprets
    the film's evocation of absence, articulated primarily in Lacanian terms,
    as resulting in a more politically oriented critique of 'the global capitalist
    culture of excess' (2007, p. 54).

Bibliography

Acord, Lance (2004) 'Filmmaker's Forum: Channeling Tokyo for "Lost in Translation"', *American Cinematographer*, vol. LXXXV, issue 1, accessed online via the FIAF International Index to Film Perioricals, fiaf.chadwyk. com/home/do.

Axmaker, Sean (2003) 'Little is "Lost in Translation" about friendship', 12 September, accessed via seattlepi.nwsource.com.

Bainbridge, Caroline (2008) *A Feminine Cinematics: Luce Irigaray, Women and Film*, Palgrave Macmillan, Basingstoke.

Barker, Martin with Thomas Austin (2000) *From Antz to Titanic: Reinventing Film Studies*, Pluto Press, London.

Barker, Martin and Kate Brooks (1998) *Knowing Audiences: Judge Dredd, Its Friends, Fans and Foes*, University of Luton Press, Luton.

Bing, Jonathan (2003) 'Where Are All the Grown-Ups?', *Variety*, 2 November, posted at variety.com.

Block, Bruce (2008) *The Visual Story: Creating the Visual Structure of Film, TV and Digital Media*, Focal Press, Burlington, MA.

Bolton, Lucy (2006) 'The Camera as Speculum: Examining Female Consciousness in *Lost in Translation*, Using the Thought of Luce Irigaray', in Renzi, Barbara Gabriella and Stephen Rainey (eds), *From Plato's Cave to the Multiplex: Contemporary Philosophy and Film*, Cambridge Scholars Press, Newcastle.

Bordwell, David (1985a) *Narration in the Fiction Film*, Routledge, London.

Bordwell, David (1985b) 'Part One: The Classical Hollywood Style, 1917–60', in Bordwell, David, Janet Staiger and Kristin Thompson, *The Classical Hollywood Cinema: Film Style and Mode of Production to 1960*, Routledge, London.

Bordwell, David (2006) *The Way Hollywood Tells It: Story and Style in Modern Movies*, California University Press, Berkeley.

Bordwell, David (2008) 'Three Dimensions of Film Narrative', in *Poetics of Cinema*, Routledge, New York and London.

Bourdieu, Pierre (1984) *Distinction: A Social Critique of the Judgement of Taste*, Routledge, London.

Bourdieu, Pierre (1993) 'The Field of Cultural Production, or; The Economic World Reversed', in *The Field of Cultural Production*, Polity Press, Cambridge.

Brooks, Brian (2003a) 'The Land of the Rising Box Office Shines Bright for "Lost in Translation"', September, accessed via indiewire.com.

Brooks, Brian (2003b) '"Scarface" Lashes the B.O.; Docs Continue Strong', September, accessed via indiewire.com.

Brownfield, Paul (2004) 'The Oscars: 76th Annual Academy Awards; The Iconoclast; What about Bill?', *Los Angeles Times*, 29 February, accessed via latimes.com.

Burr, Ty (2003) 'Lost in Translation Movie Review', 12 September, accessed via boston.com.

Caro, Mark (2003) 'Movie Review: "Lost in Translation"', 11 September, accessed via Chicago.metromix.com.

Charney, Leo (1998) *Empty Moments: Cinema, Modernity, and Drift*, NC: Duke University Press, Durham.

Cheng, Scarlet (2003) 'Fall Sneaks; Though Western eyes', *Los Angeles Times*, Sunday Calendar, 7 September, accessed via latimes.com.

Chion, Michel (1994) *Audio-Vision: Sound on Screen*, Columbia University Press, New York.

Clark, John (2003) 'Holiday Sneaks; Young heart and old soul', *Los Angeles Times*, 9 November, accessed via latimes.com.

Clark, Mike (2003) 'Comedy Doesn't Get Lost in "Translation"', 12 September, accessed via usatoday.com.

Colman, Felicity J. (2005) 'Cinema: Movement-Image-Recognition-Time', in Charles J. Stivale (ed.), *Gilles Deleuze: Key Concepts*, McGill-Queen's University Press, Montreal.

Crabtree, Sheigh (2003) 'Editor Flack in Fashion for Coppola's "Lost" Pic', *The Hollywood Reporter*, 10 September, accessed via thehollywoodreporter.com.

Day, Kiku (2004) 'Totally lost in translation', *The Guardian*, 24 January, accessed via guardian.co.uk.

De Vany, Arthur (2004) *Hollywood Economics: How Extreme Uncertainty Shapes the Film Industry*, Routledge, London.

Diaconescu, Sorina (2001) 'Fall Sneaks; an upstart, casual but confident; Filmmaker Sofia Coppola lets intuition be her creative guide', *Los Angeles Times*, E.20, 7 September, accessed via latimes.com

Dyer, Richard (1997) *White*, Routledge, London.

Ebert, Roger (2003) 'Lost in Translation', *Chicago Sun-Times*, 12 September, accessed via suntimes.com.

Elder, Sean (2001) 'Bill Murray', *Salon.com*, 6 February, accessed via salon.com.

Evans, Peter and Celestino Deleyto (eds) (1998) *Terms of Endearment: Hollywood Romantic Comedy of the 1980s and 1990s*, Edinburgh University Press, Edinburgh.

Fonarow, Wendy (2006) *Empire of Dirt: The Aesthetics and Rituals of British Indie Music*, Wesleyan University Press, Middletown, CT.

Grove, Martin A. (2003a) 'Focus Heads Focus on "Translation" Success', *The Hollywood Reporter*, 10 October, accessed via thehollywoodreporter.com.

Grove, Martin A. (2003b) 'Word is terrific for Coppola's "Translation"', *The Hollywood Reporter*, 15 August, accessed via thehollywoodreporter.com.

Grove, Martin A. (2004a) 'Academy Members Have Thrown Dice or Thrown Away Votes', *The Hollywood Reporter*, 16 January, accessed via thehollywoodreporter.com.

Grove, Martin (2004b) 'Forever Oscar', *The Hollywood Reporter*, 27 February, accessed via thehollywoodreporter.com.

Gunning, Tom (1990) 'The Cinema of Attractions: Early Film, Its Spectator and the Avant-Garde', in Elsaesser, Thomas (ed.), *Early Cinema: Space/Frame/Narrative*, BFI, London.

Guthmann, Edward (2003) 'The message is loud and clear in "Lost in Translation"', *San Francisco Chronicle*, 12 September, accessed via sfgate.com.

Hale, Mike (2004) 'Film: This Week; A Pair of Nonidentical Twins', *The New York Times*, 1 August, accessed via nytimes.com.

Harris, Dana and Cathy Dunkley, (2003) 'Focus Frames "Lost" Deal at Finish of AFM', *Variety*, 25 February, posted at variety.com.

Harris, Dana (2003) 'New film legends of the fall', *Variety*, 12 October, posted at variety.com.

Harvey, David (1991) *The Condition of Postmodernity: An Enquiry into the Origins of Cultural Change*, Blackwell, Oxford.

Heffernan, Virginia (2003) 'The New Season/Film; Scarlet Johansson, Indie Ingénue And Expert Lolita', *New York Times*, 7 September, accessed via nytimes.com.

Hettrick, Scott (2004) '"Lost" Translates to DVD, Bigscreen', 17 February, posted at variety.com.

Hirschberg, Lynn (1999) 'Bill Murray, in all seriousness', *The New York Times* magazine, 31 January, accessed via nytimes.com.

Hirschberg, Lynn (2003) 'The Coppola Smart Mob', *The New York Times*, magazine, 31 August, accessed via nytimes.com.

Hohenadel, Kristen (2006) 'French Royalty as seen by Hollywood Royalty', *The New York Times*, 10 September, accessed via nytimes.com.

Honeycutt, Kirk (2003) 'Lost in Translation', *The Hollywood Reporter*, 2 September, accessed via thehollywoodreporter.com.

Honeycutt, Kirk (2006) 'Riding Alone for Miles', *The Hollywood Reporter*, 1 September, accessed via thehollywoodreporter.com.

Hundley, Jessica (2003) 'POP MUSIC; An invisible role; Brian Reitzell's music is a key character in "Lost in Translation"', *Los Angeles Times*, 11 September, accessed via latimes.com.

Karnick, Kristine and Henry Jenkins (eds) (1995) *Classical Hollywood Comedy*, Routledge, New York.

Kern, Stephen (2003) *The Culture of Time and Space, 1880–1918*, Harvard University Press, Cambridge, MA.

King, Barry (1991) 'Articulating Stardom', in Gledhill, Christine (ed.), *Stardom: Industry of Desire*, Routledge, London.

King, Geoff (2000) *Spectacular Narratives: Hollywood in the Age of the Blockbuster*, I. B. Tauris, London.

King, Geoff (2002a) *Film Comedy*, Wallflower Press, London.

King, Geoff (2002b) *New Hollywood Cinema: An Introduction*, I. B. Tauris, London.

King, Geoff (2004) 'Weighing Up the Qualities of Independence: *21 Grams* in Focus', *Film Studies: An International Review*, 5.

King, Geoff (2005) *American Independent Cinema*, London, I. B.Tauris.

King, Geoff (2007) *Donnie Darko*, Wallflower Press, London.

King, Geoff (2009) *Indiewood USA: Where Hollywood Meets Independent Cinema*, I. B. Tauris, London.

Klevan, Andrew (2000) *Disclosure of the Everyday: Undramatic Achievement in Narrative Film*, Flicks Books, Trowbridge, Wilts.

Kolker, Robert Philip (1982) *The Altering Eye: Contemporary International Cinema*, Oxford University Press, Oxford.

Kovács, András Bálint (2007) *Screening Modernism: European Art Cienma, 1950–1980*, University of Chicago Press, Chicago and London.

Lewis, Reina (1996) *Gendering Orientalism: Race, Femininity and Representation*, Routledge, London.

Littlewood, Ian (1996) *The Idea of Japan: Western Images, Western Myths*. Secker and Warburg, London.

Lumenick, Lou (2003) 'Fits the Bill: Cheers to Murray & Co. for the Sublime "Lost in Translation"', 12 September, accessed via nypost.com.

Mayne, Judith (1990) *The Woman at the Keyhole: Feminism and Women's Cinema*, Indiana University Press, Bloomington.

McGowan, Todd (2007) 'There Is Nothing *Lost in Translation*', *Quarterly Review of Film and Video*, 24.

Meyer, Carla (2003) 'Sofia Coppola has a little humor and, now, a big film. Father Francis and husband Spike? Not a factor', *San Francisco Chronicle*, 20 September, accessed via sfgate.com.

Mitchell, Elvis (2003) 'Film Review; An American in Japan, Making a Connection', 12 September, accessed via nytimes.com.

Mitchell, Elvis (2004) 'Critic's Notebook; Best Film Bellwether Goes to Spirit Awards', *The New York Times*, 27 February, accessed via nytimes.com.

Mitchell, Wendy (2003) 'Sofia Coppola Talks About "Lost in Translation", Her Love Story That's Not "Nerdy"', *indieWIRE*, no date, accessed via indiewire.com.

Musetto, V. A. (2004) '"Lost" in Transition – Japan Critics Rip Flick', *New York Post*, 21 May, accessed via nypost.com.

Neale, Steve (2000) *Genre and Hollywood*, Routledge, London.

Perkins, V. F. (1972) *Film as Film*, Penguin, Harmondsworth.

Purdie, Susan (1993) *Comedy: The Mastery of Discourse*, Harvester Wheatsheaf, New York.

Rich, Motoko (2004) 'Land of the Rising Cliché', *The New York Times*, 4 January, accessed via nytimes.com.

Rooney, David (2003) 'Lost in Translation', *Variety*, 31 August, posted at variety.com.

Saccone, Melinda (2004) 'Coppola's "Translation" Translates Well to Video', *Home Media Magazine*, 13 February, accessed via www.homemediamag azine.com/news/coppolas-translation-translates-well-to-video-5858.

Said, Edward (1978) *Orientalism: Western Conceptions of the Orient*, Routledge, London.

Sarris, Andrew (1981) 'Notes on the Auteur Theory in 1962', in Caughie, John (ed.), *Theories of Authorship*, Routledge, London.

Scott, A. O. (2003) 'Film; Murray's Art of Losing', *The New York Times*, 14 September, accessed via nytimes.com.

Seidman, Steve (1979) *Comedian Comedy: A Tradition in Hollywood Film*, UMI Research Press, Ann Arbor, MI.

Siegel, Tatiana (2009) 'Sofia books Marmont film', *Variety*, 16 April, posted at variety.com.

Smith, Murray (1995) *Engaging Characters: Fiction, Emotion and the Cinema*, Clarendon Press, Oxford.

Snyder, Gabriel (2004) 'Niche Pics Lost in a Big Crowd', *Variety*, 1 July, posted at variety.com.

Thompson, Anne (2003) 'Tokyo Story', *Filmmaker*, Fall, accessed via www.filmmakermagazine.com.

Thompson, Kristin (1999) *Storytelling in the New Hollywood: Understanding Classical Narrative Technique*, Harvard University Press, Cambridge, MA.

Turan, Kenneth (2003) 'Movie Review: "Lost in Translation"', 12 September, accessed via www.calanderlive.com/movies.

Tzioumakis, Yannis (2006) *American Independent Cinema: An Introduction*, Edinburgh University Press, Edinburgh.

Variety Staff, (2003) 'Weekend Box Office Preview September 12, 2003', *Variety*, 11 September, posted at variety.com.

Wright, George (2004) 'Hit film gets lost in racism row', *The Guardian*, 27 February, posted at guardian.co.uk.

Wyatt, Justin (1998) 'The formation of the "major independent": Miramax, New Line and the New Hollywood', in Neale, Steve, and Murray Smith (eds), *Contemporary Hollywood Cinema*, London and Routledge, New York.

Zacharek, Stephanie (2003) 'Lost in Translation', 12 September, accessed via www.salon.com.

Index